TWENTIETH CENTURY
INTERPRETATIONS
OF
THE OLD MAN
AND THE SEA

A Collection of Critical Essays

Edited by
KATHARINE T. JOBES

Prentice-Hall, Inc.   *Englewood Cliffs, N. J.*

A SPECTRUM BOOK

Current printing (last number):

10 9 8 7 6 5 4 3 2 1

Prentice-Hall International, Inc. (*London*)

Acknowledgments

The editor is grateful to the authors and publishers who generously permitted their work to appear in this anthology and to Tilden G. Edelstein, Forrest C. Jobes, Jr., Elliot L. Rubenstein, and David R. Weimer for their helpful suggestions about the manuscript.

Katharine T. Jobes

Contents

Contents

Introduction

by Katharine T. Jobes

I

By 1952, when *The Old Man and the Sea* was published, Ernest Hemingway needed to make a big catch. He had not made one since *For Whom the Bell Tolls* in 1940. Much of his literary reputation rested on works written between 1924 and 1933. His energetic participation in World War II as a correspondent (he is supposed to have entered Paris before the Allied occupation forces) had not yielded the literary results of his earlier experience in World War I (*A Farewell to Arms*, 1929) or the Spanish Civil War (*For Whom the Bell Tolls*)—only *Across the River and Into the Trees* (1950), a novel received with almost unanimous critical dismay at the author's unintentional self-parody.

The Old Man and the Sea appeared at first to restore public confidence in Hemingway's championship. With few exceptions, critics in both popular and scholarly publications hailed it enthusiastically, concurring with the publisher's pronouncement on the dust jacket that it was a "new classic" and comparing it favorably with a wide range of more seasoned classics like "The Bear," *Moby Dick*, "The Ancient Mariner," *King Lear*, and "The Seafarer." It occasioned an impressive list of awards, including the Pulitzer Prize for fiction (May 4, 1953) and the Award of Merit Medal for the Novel given by the American Academy of Arts and Letters. Hemingway received the Nobel Prize for Literature in 1954, " 'for his powerful, style-forming mastery of the art of modern narration, as most recently evinced in "The Old Man and the Sea." ' " [1]

Since the initial extravagant praise, however, a dissenting strain of criticism has arisen as well, providing counterpoint to less extravagant, but continuing praise. Philip Young's second thoughts in *Ernest Hemingway: A Reconsideration* (1966) about his own evaluation of 1952 (see pp. 25–26 below) typify the shift away from almost unqualified enthusiasm. Although Carlos Baker calls it "major" in the

---

[1] *New York Times*, Oct. 29, 1954, Sec. I, p. 1:4.

1

title of his critical anthology *Ernest Hemingway: Critiques of Four Major Novels* (1962), other critics, including some like Leslie Fiedler and Norman Mailer who have profound respect for Hemingway's early work,[2] find *The Old Man and the Sea* a disappointing minor work.

The reader will want to consider how a work which has been widely praised as a "classic" and "masterpiece" and which continues to enjoy wide popularity, according to the evidence of its sales,[3] can also be attacked as "fakery" and "fraud," as "imitation Hemingway." Both attitudes are represented in this collection; the reader should judge both in the light of his own reading of *The Old Man and the Sea*.

II

One of the first things the reader will notice is that despite the marked division of critical opinion, there is surprisingly little disagreement about the meaning of *The Old Man and the Sea* or about the techniques by which Hemingway expresses it.[4] The disagreement comes in evaluation rather than explication.

Most explicators agree that Hemingway's theme, expressed in the apparently simple, yet actually intricately designed plot of Santiago's adventure with the marlin and sharks, is man's capacity to withstand and transcend hardships of time and circumstance. Hemingway depicts in circumstantial detail elemental tests of endurance (physical struggle, fatigue, solitude, old age, impending death) to which Santiago is subjected, and also his courageous response, summoning both physical energy and imaginative vision to counter the forces testing him. When the marlin takes out line, Santiago pulls in; when he is surrounded by the darkness of night, Santiago dreams of golden and white beaches; when he is threatened by the weakness of old age, he summons visions of his own youthful strength. Hemingway presents the action not in abstract terms—gain and loss, strength and weakness, youth and age—but in vivid images—marlin and shark, right hand and left, Manolin and Santiago.

[2] Fiedler, p. 108 below, and *No! in Thunder* (Boston: Beacon, 1960), pp. 17–18. Mailer, *Advertisements for Myself* (New York: Berkley, 1959), pp. 18–19.

[3] *The New York Times Book Review*, Feb. 25, 1968, Sec. VII, Part 2, p. 26, lists a Scribner's report of 275,000 paperback sales in 1967. This figure greatly exceeds the figure of 150,000 paperback copies each given by Scribner's in the same list for Hemingway's *The Sun Also Rises* and *A Farewell to Arms*, novels favored by disparagers of *The Old Man and the Sea*.

[4] The most substantial disagreement is on whether or not *The Old Man and the Sea* is a tragedy. For discussion see the Gurko-Burhans-Sylvester sequence reprinted below and the Rovit View Point below.

Hemingway reflects the central action of the story, which is Santiago's trial by the marlin and sharks, in a number of miniature actions. Some, incidents appropriate to the sea setting, anticipate the pattern of the central chase. The episode of the man-of-war bird resolutely but unsuccessfully chasing flying fish[5] suggests Santiago's coming effort to land his great winged fish. The tired warbler threatened by hawks on his way in to shore (pp. 54–56) predicts the tired Santiago's trial by sharks. Others, sketches of heroic human action, show how man at his best can respond to natural stresses like those of the chase. To keep his will strong and to inspire his best effort, Santiago recalls his morning victory after the difficult night of his twenty-four-hour handwrestling contest with the Negro from Cienfuegos. He emulates the great DiMaggio, who plays like a champion despite the pain of a bone spur. Hemingway evokes the climactic model of tested and transcendent heroism, surpassing the models Santiago envisions for himself, in the crucifixion imagery he uses to describe Santiago's suffering.

Interdependence of the central and secondary actions is indicated by interlocking imagery. Santiago comments, for example, after fighting the two shovel-nosed sharks: "If I could have used a *bat* with two hands I could have killed the first one surely" (p. 114; italics added). The noble marlin's sword is "as long as a baseball bat" (p. 62) and has perhaps been used as a weapon against sharks (p. 115). Santiago's traitorous left hand is associated with destructive creatures like the hawk which may be awaiting the tired warbler: "his left hand was still as tight as the gripped claws of an eagle" (p. 63). The teeth of the mako shark, in turn, are "shaped like a man's fingers when they are crisped like claws" (pp. 100–1).

The repeated images are part of a pervasive and emphatic stylistic design of repeated sounds, words, rhythms, and grammatical patterns, all of which reinforce the structural design of related actions. The style often has the quality of incantation, giving to even routine actions the dignity of ritual.

The bóy was sad tóo and we bégged her párdon and butchered her prómptly.

(p. 50; emphasis added)

Báck in the bów he laid the two fíllets of físh oút on the wood with the

---

[5] Ernest Hemingway, *The Old Man and the Sea,* The Scribner Library (New York: Charles Scribner's Sons, 1952), pp. 33–34. All subsequent references to *The Old Man and the Sea* are to this edition and will be cited parenthetically in the text. Page references to *The Old Man and the Sea* in all Essays and View Points have been standardized to this edition.

flying fish beside them.

(p. 79; emphasis added)

He looked up at the sky and then out to his fish.

(p. 96; emphasis added)

"He is tiring or he is resting," . . . .

(p. 79; emphasis added)

Both narrator and hero perceive the stresses and responses of the action in a pattern of natural ritual. They see victor and victim as part of a natural and inevitable continuum of pursuing and being pursued. The dolphin pursues and catches the flying fish and is in turn caught by the old man, who is nourished by the victim fish so that he can catch a bigger fish. The victor is in his turn victimized by big fish, sharks, while sharks in their turn are destroyed by man for man's advantage. (Note the reference to the shark factory, p. 11, and to the fishermen's drinking shark liver oil for medicinal purposes, p. 37.) First Santiago is victor over the marlin; then he suffers vicariously the marlin's defeat as the sharks strip away its flesh. To live with equanimity is to recognize and accept the natural rhythms in which man participates. Santiago reflects, as the strike of the first shark threatens to turn his victory into defeat, "everything kills everything else in some way" (p. 106).

For an individual to be the victim in this natural struggle is no disgrace if he fights well according to his gifts. To lose eventually is inevitable. But the noble creatures in the story—the marlin, the mako shark, the turtle with its lasting heart, all of which are identified in some way with Santiago—transcend defeat by displaying intense life at the moment of death, as if releasing their vital force to a successor. In this context, we can understand Santiago's climactic statement, " 'A man can be destroyed but not defeated' " (p. 103).

Hemingway's elaborate narrative design, static and tapestry-like, with its basic pattern repeated in variations and intertwinings, invites us to share Santiago's reflective temper, to contemplate the *meaning* of the action, rather than be caught up in it for its own sake. We can sense through the wounds and blood and sharks' teeth a natural and harmonious ritual in which the eating of the victim's flesh provides continuing vitality to the victor. From the act of killing and eating his totem-brother, Santiago *becomes* the marlin. Imaginatively he assimilates vital nourishment from his human brothers—the powerful Negro from Cienfuegos, DiMaggio, the boy Manolin, his own earlier self. In every case, for loss there is gain; for sacrifice, recompense. The obverse of Santiago's "everything kills everything else" is that everything nourishes everything else in some way.

This principle of physical or spiritual assimilation, which we might call the conservation of vitality, makes possible the triumphant resolution of the rhythms of the story. The final scene takes place at morning, after Santiago's night of trial by the sharks. Santiago, who has slept in cruciform position, is resurrected from his sense of being beaten and plans with the boy the shaping of a new lance. Although he is asleep again at the very end, Santiago "was dreaming" about the lions. The verb tense is imperfect; the action incomplete. And even should this be his final sleep, as Bickford Sylvester contends (pp. 91–92 below) and as the transfer of the marlin's identity to Santiago might suggest, he has given the marlin's spear to the boy; hence the possibility, through a chosen and dedicated heir, and again through the process of transmitted vitality, of infinitely repeatable heroism.

Hemingway's technique of superimposing parallel heroic actions implies that the heroic ideal symbolized by Santiago can be easily generalized as well. And in a remark about his intent in *The Old Man and the Sea*, Hemingway confirms the impression given by the story itself:

> "I tried to make a real old man, a real boy, a real sea and a real fish and real sharks. But if I made them good and true enough they would mean many things." [6]

Taking Hemingway's suggestion freely, critics point out the transferability of the heroic model established by Santiago to many things partaking in the same natural rhythms—many men, many trials, many losses, many resolute comebacks from losses. Sympathetic critics find in *The Old Man and the Sea* the basic action and timelessness of a parable wherein every reader can perceive a personally meaningful image of moral heroism.

III

The Old Man and the Sea has been interpreted not only as a parable about the heroic capabilities of man in general, but also as Hemingway's private parable. Indeed part of the critical disagreement about it, as we shall see, centers upon how successfully Hemingway has made private emotional concerns expressive of the concerns of his readers.

This question has been raised about much of Hemingway's writing, since it so clearly reveals biographical origins.[7] Most critics agree

[6] "An American Storyteller," *Time*, LXIV (Dec. 13, 1954), 72.
[7] An authorized biography is in preparation by Carlos Baker.
The reader interested in the relationship between Hemingway writing and

that in the fiction of the 1920's and early 1930's, which is based upon experiences of his boyhood and young manhood, Hemingway achieved an exceptionally successful fusion of private and public expression.

Hemingway was born in Oak Park, Illinois, a suburb of Chicago, in 1899, the son of Dr. Clarence Hemingway and Grace Hall Hemingway. He was educated in Oak Park schools and spent summers with his family in the woods of upper Michigan. After his graduation from high school in 1917, he worked briefly as a reporter for the Kansas City *Star* before going to Italy as a volunteer ambulance driver for the Red Cross. On July 8, 1918, he was severely wounded by Austrian fire at Fossalta di Piave. Following a restless convalescence at home and in Michigan in 1919, he went to work as a reporter for the Toronto *Star* and *Star Weekly,* at first in Toronto, then in Paris as a foreign correspondent. In Paris he met a number of writers, among them Gertrude Stein and Ezra Pound, who encouraged his interest in creative writing, and in 1924, he gave up reporting to concentrate on his own work.

The fictional themes which Hemingway draws from his youthful experience (his heroes' experiences are markedly like his own) suggest that he found the genteel, middle-class, Protestant values of his parents and of Oak Park illusory when they were challenged by the more primitive experience of upper Michigan, the violent scenes of his Kansas City police station and hospital beats, and the horrors of war on the Italian front, particularly the climactic shock of his own wounding. Expatriation appears in the fiction as alienation from Oak Park-like values; rituals based on physical action in nature (hunting, fishing, bullfighting—all of which Hemingway himself pursued expertly) as workable replacements for illusory ordering rites based on idealism or supernaturalism.

The troubling shocks and responses of Hemingway's own youth proved immediately significant to his entire generation, which had collectively suffered a painful coming of age, and more generally to any generation, as the enduring place in modern literature of *In Our Time, The Sun Also Rises,* and *A Farewell to Arms* attests. Heming-

---

biography should consult such critical studies as Baker's *Hemingway: The Writer as Artist,* 3rd ed. (Princeton: Princeton University Press, 1963); Charles A. Fenton, *The Apprenticeship of Ernest Hemingway: The Early Years* (New York: Farrar, Straus & Giroux, Inc., 1954); and Philip Young, *Ernest Hemingway: A Reconsideration* (University Park: The Pennsylvania State University Press, 1966).

Memoirs by Hemingway's brother and sister give an idea of the genteel atmosphere in the Hemingway family and in the Oak Park of Ernest Hemingway's youth: Leicester Hemingway, *My Brother, Ernest Hemingway* (Cleveland: World Publishing Co., 1962); Marcelline (Hemingway) Sanford, *At the Hemingways: A Family Portrait* (Boston: Little, Brown and Company, 1962).

way's own generation had been profoundly shocked by its engagement with European experience in World War I and by the failure of Wilsonian idealism. His fictional representation of the inadequacies of conventional values appealed to many young people for whom nineteenth-century American small-town values were no longer viable in the complex twentieth-century world of industrialization, urbanization, and mass warfare. The war wounds of Hemingway's heroes recalled the generational wound of World War I or youthful vulnerability at large. Their "separate peace" or post-war expatriation dramatized the spiritual alienation of many youthful Americans from the official values of their country. Their rituals appealed, directly or symbolically, to many who could no longer believe in old forms of order in their apparently disordered social world.

Hemingway's prose style, too, spoke to the need of his generation. From laconic conversational rhythms and from the journalistic prose in which he served his apprenticeship, he developed a spare prose, characterized by concrete nouns, few coloring adjectives or literary figures, limited range of vocabulary, and elementary sentence structure. He designed this style to do what nineteenth-century realists had attempted to do with precisely recorded regional dialects—to express things the way they really are. The impression of terse factuality, objectivity, and emotional control carried over from the journalistic origins of the prose represents a reaction against the rhetoric of the Oak Park world of illusions. The "news" of his time, not traditional dogma, is what Hemingway wished to convey.[8]

The successful merging of public and private proved more difficult for Hemingway to achieve in his later fiction. Not surprisingly, since private experiences and emotions are essential to his fiction, Hemingway appears to have confused celebration of the early fiction, in which his historical self is transcended and made general in significance by self-critical selection and shaping, with celebration of his private personality. In the 1930's, he turned to exploiting the personal legend of Hemingway, becoming openly his own hero in *Death in the Afternoon, Green Hills of Africa,* and a series of letters to *Esquire* magazine. Writing in his own person, Hemingway lacks the quality of defensive reticence so appealing in his early fictional heroes. He

---

[8] Hemingway's sense of the "news" of his disordered time is reflected in the cover design of his second published volume, *in our time* (Paris, 1924)—a montage of fragments of news headlines from around the world. His sense of shared experience is reflected in the plural pronoun "our" in the title. Philip Young suggests that the title, in addition to pointing to contemporary materials representative of twentieth-century experience, is probably a sardonic allusion to "Give us peace in our time, O Lord," from the Book of Common Prayer. *Ernest Hemingway: A Reconsideration,* p. 30.

tends to flaunt personal emotion and, snobbishly, to make of sporting technique (a central concern in the writing of this period) a cult of expertise, rather than an emblem of tenuous defense against disorder, as in his fiction.

But if Hemingway overemphasized the importance of his own personality, his critics on their part overemphasized his public duty. Many of them formulated his success at expressing an important mood of the 1920's into a conception of Hemingway as social critic with an obligation to use his art for the public good. Critics who had praised his wounded and alienated heroes as an indictment of complacent small-town America returned in the 1930's from their own expatriation. They castigated Hemingway for publicizing frivolous personal tastes such as bullfighting and fishing and demanded of him (often in Marxist terminology) a literature of serious social engagement for the new *our time* of the depression '30's.

Chastened, perhaps, by such criticism, or converted by his interest in the Loyalist cause in the Spanish Civil War, Hemingway made at least some concession to social concern in the subject matter and themes of *To Have and Have Not* (1937), *The Fifth Column* (1938), and *For Whom the Bell Tolls* (1940). But the artistic cost of social dutifulness shows in the structural weaknesses and stilted dialogue which mar even *For Whom the Bell Tolls,* by far the best of the three works. Perhaps partly in reaction to the artistic difficulties of this period, Hemingway returned in *Across the River and Into the Trees* (1950) to fiction superficially more like the successful early pattern of alienated heroes gallantly constructing fragile private defenses against disorder. But this time the alienated hero, Colonel Cantwell, appears so crotchety and self-indulgent as to render the novel, for all the interest of its structure and theme, an unfortunate parody of the early fiction, in which alienation is regarded with sadness rather than self-congratulation. Hemingway, who is reported to have thought this novel his best,[9] suffered even greater critical chastisement than in the self-as-hero 1930's for self-indulgence in the thin fictional guise of Colonel Cantwell. It was in this hostile critical climate that he wrote *The Old Man and the Sea.*

Santiago's story has been widely interpreted as a symbolic representation of Hemingway's vision of himself in 1952.[10] The typical

[9] Lillian Ross, *Portrait of Hemingway* (New York: Simon & Schuster, 1961), p. 25. (Originally published as a *New Yorker* Profile, May 13, 1950.)

[10] The first of many biographical readings appeared in a *Life* editorial, p. 20, accompanying the first publication of *The Old Man and the Sea, Life,* XXXIII (Sept. 1, 1952), 35–54:

It is often highbrow practice to find symbolism in Hemingway's work. *The Old Man and the Sea* seems perfect to us as it stands; but for those who like biographical reading identifies Santiago—the meticulous craftsman dedicated to his vocation—with Hemingway as writer; and Santiago's faded reputation as champion with Hemingway's literary reputation in the early 1950's. Santiago's suffering from the loss of his agonizingly won big fish to the sharks allegedly dramatizes Hemingway's suffering from critics' attacks on *Across the River and Into the Trees,* in which his ego, particularly his fear of aging and dying, was deeply engaged. Or, more generally, the sharks are said to stand for all the forces, external or internal, which work against the craftsman's achievement of unchallenged championship.

The pattern of Hemingway's career as literary craftsman in his last decade supports the theory that *The Old Man and the Sea* dramatizes an intense personal conviction. Hemingway began after 1950 to practice the technique of envisioning his youthful self, which he depicts as revitalizing the aged champion Santiago. As if to regain the strength of his own youthful championship, both in writing and in sports, Hemingway returned in fact and in fictional setting to the scenes of his greatest triumphs.[11] In reverse of the original temporal order, fighting against ongoing time, he returned during his residence in Cuba (and in *The Old Man and the Sea*) to the days of championship deep-sea fishing and *Esquire* articles in the 1930's; then to Africa on safari and to Spain for bullfighting. But literary revitalization proved as elusive as the great marlin he tried (as if he imagined himself literally Santiago) unsuccessfully to catch for the Hollywood filming

---

a little symbolism, we have tried to deduce some. Perhaps the old man is Hemingway himself, the great fish is this great story and the sharks are the critics. Symbolism won't match up to real life here, though: there is absolutely nothing the sharks can do to this marlin.

Life furthered the identification by printing on p. 34, facing the first page of the text of the story, a full page photograph of Hemingway against the background of "a Cuban fishing village like the one used by the 'old man' of his story." In the Letters to the Editors section, Sept. 22, 1952, p. 12, *Life* printed a photograph of Hemingway beside a half-eaten marlin which he had landed.

Hemingway may himself have fostered the tendency of some critics to identify him with his hero. The imagery of his response to the Nobel award in 1954 can be read as suggesting a spiritual identification of himself with Santiago:

"How simple the writing of literature would be if it were only necessary to write in another way what has been well written. It is because we have had such great writers in the past that a writer is driven far out past where he can go, out to where no one can help him."

New York Times, Dec. 11, 1954, Sec. I., p. 5:2.

[11] This pattern is commented on by Carlos Baker, "Introduction" in *Hemingway and His Critics: An International Anthology,* American Century Series (New York: Hill and Wang, 1961), pp. 11–12; and by Leslie Fiedler, *Waiting for the End* (New York: Stein and Day, 1964), p. 16.

of *The Old Man and the Sea*. After 1952, his search produced only
two works of substance. "The Dangerous Summer," a study of bullfighting published by *Life* in 1960, has not appeared in book form.
The excellent *A Moveable Feast* (1964), which, barring other posthu-
mous publication, seems the only lasting work after *The Old Man
and the Sea*, is based on notes written much earlier. The essays in *A
Moveable Feast*, which Hemingway worked over in his last months,
return in subject matter and setting to the days in Paris in the 1920's
when he was first winning his literary championship. Perhaps Hemingway's suicide on July 2, 1961, was a return even further back in time
to the traumatic July, 1918, of his youthful war wounds. The ideal
of transcendent championship which he had represented in Santiago
in 1952 proved visionary for Hemingway himself.

How the pressure of Hemingway's personal emotions, as he perhaps anticipated the difficult struggle which marked his last decade,
affects the success of *The Old Man and the Sea* as a parable about
human heroism generally provides one of the issues of debate about
the story. Admirers feel that Hemingway matches the success of the
early fiction in making his private concern publicly relevant, so that
his readers can share his emotional investment in the novel.[12] In
Santiago, he has created a hero through whom he can explore the
stresses of aging and impending death which preoccupied him in *Across
the River and Into the Trees*, as well as the stress of threatened championship, but from whom he can maintain critical distance, thus
avoiding the cultism and special pleading which mar the 1950 novel.
The elemental simplicity of the humble Cuban fisherman and his adventure, which separates him clearly from any direct and literal identification with his complex creator, also fits him to serve as a symbolic
type of common human experience.

Opposing critics argue that Hemingway's private emotional need
caused him to violate the integrity of Santiago's story. They point out
particularly his distortion of the circumstantial detail upon which
much of the effectiveness of the story depends, detail which Hemingway, himself a champion deep-sea fisherman, presumably knew. Philip
Young attributes the distortion to Hemingway's private allegorical
endeavor (see p. 26 below); Robert Weeks to Hemingway's desire to
believe in an orderly universe (see pp. 39–40 below). To the extent
that one is troubled by such distortions, *The Old Man and the Sea*
may seem less persuasive as a universal parable.

[12] See, for example, Sheridan Baker, *Ernest Hemingway: An Introduction and
Interpretation*, American Authors and Critics Series (New York: Holt, Rinehart,
& Winston, 1967), pp. 126, 128; and Young, pp. 21–22 below.

IV

The particular case of the biographical criticism, in which critics agree substantially in their readings, yet disagree conspicuously in their evaluations (Philip Young in 1966 even disagreed with his own 1952 evaluation) introduces a general problem involved in assessing much of the criticism of *The Old Man and the Sea*. A statement like Philip Toynbee's "You either believe or you do not believe that the book is meretricious from beginning to end . . ." (p. 112 below) may sound like abdication of critical responsibility. But the more one studies the criticism of *The Old Man and the Sea,* the more one agrees with Toynbee. *The Old Man and the Sea* seems particularly susceptible to contradictory judgments based upon the same textual evidence. Take, for example, Hemingway's evocation of crucifixion: " '*Ay*,' he said aloud. There is no translation for this word and perhaps it is just a noise such as a man might make, involuntarily, feeling the nail go through his hands and into the wood" (p. 107). This passage can be judged favorably (or at least neutrally) as functional in extending the significance of Santiago's agony (Wells, p. 61 below, and Introduction, p. 3 above); or it can be judged unfavorably as obtrusive encouragement of what Philip Rahv calls "inflationary readings" (p. 111 below). Earl Rovit calls it "distinctly artificial and obtrusive." [13] The description of Santiago's fishing lines as being "thick around as a big pencil" (p. 31) can be seen as a useful clue linking Santiago's craft symbolically with Hemingway's, or as a damaging violation of credibility caused by the distorting pressure of Hemingway's autobiographical interest. (See Young on the "gaffe," p. 26 below.) Santiago's baseball talk, considered helpful by Philip Young and Clinton Burhans in establishing character, tone, and theme (pp. 23–24 and 76–77 below) is considered by Claire Rosenfield damaging, because of its triviality, to the serious treatment of ritual in the story (pp. 41–42 below). The prose style, praised for its lucidity by Malcolm Cowley (p. 107 below) is censured by Philip Toynbee for insufferable "archaic false simplicities" (p. 112 below).

Such specific disagreements—and the reader will find more—point to differences in general critical tastes and attitudes which divide those who like *The Old Man and the Sea* from those who do not. Robert Weeks and Bickford Sylvester disagree, for example, about Hemingway's accuracy in matters of naturalistic detail. The pattern of natural

---

[13] *Ernest Hemingway,* Twayne's United States Authors Series (New York: Twayne, 1963), p. 90.

rhythm created by Hemingway's meticulous linking of detail, which Sylvester points out in his defense of the novel ("Hemingway's Extended Vision . . . ," reprinted below), is regarded by Weeks as fakery based on distortion or falsification of natural facts in the interest of simulating a "cozy" or "warm" universe, a betrayal of Hemingway's principle of telling things as they are ("Fakery in *The Old Man and the Sea*," reprinted below). Weeks expects Hemingway to be a realist. He discusses the related thematic and ethical functions of realism in Hemingway's early fiction; he cites Hemingway's specific concern for making a *real* old man, fish, and sea in *The Old Man and the Sea*. Sylvester, responding explicitly to Weeks, defends Hemingway's right to symbolic poetic license in his presentation of a mature "extended vision" of man's participation in the rhythms of an orderly universe. ". . . 'the way it was' need no longer be his sole guide as an artist" (p. 95 below). Should the integrity of a theme presented by means of circumstantial detail of physical objects and actions be judged according to the factual accuracy of those details? Or should the theme itself, regarded as an ideal vision, take precedence over factuality? To critics of Weeks' persuasion, the very term "ideal vision" represents a betrayal of Hemingway's original moral and aesthetic revolution, a retrogression to the illusory values he left in leaving Oak Park. But to Sylvester the affirmative sense of order in *The Old Man and the Sea* testifies to Hemingway's evolution toward a new philosophical maturity.

Weeks and Sylvester agree, despite their difference on the matter of realism, that *The Old Man and the Sea* reveals a new Hemingway. Not all critics concur. One strain of negative criticism argues that it is simply old Hemingway réchauffé. Dwight Macdonald calls it "simply his early short story, 'The Undefeated,' perhaps the best thing he ever did, re-told in terms of fishing instead of bullfighting and transposed from a spare, austere style into a slack, fake-biblical style which retains the mannerisms and omits the virtues. . . ." [14] Leslie Fiedler feels that "Hemingway is no longer creating, but merely imitating the marvelous spare style that was once a revelation" (p. 108 below). According to the point of view represented by these critics, it is not sufficient for Hemingway to imitate old performances. His early literary revolution has already been consolidated by Hemingway himself and by a host of imitators. To retain his literary championship he must create a new aesthetic and ethic for a new "our time" in order not to betray the revolutionary essence of his ideal self.

From the hints given by these examples, one suspects—and the suspicion has some support in the evidence of Hemingway's critics'

[14] "Ernest Hemingway," *Encounter*, XVIII (January, 1962), 121.

tastes and attitudes appearing in their writing, critical or creative, on subjects other than Hemingway[15]—that opinion about *The Old Man and the Sea* is divided according to broad critical attitudes extrinsic to the work itself and to Hemingway's work as a whole. Those who praise *The Old Man and the Sea* incline to an attitude rooted in humanistic or Transcendental intellectual tradition.[16] They are centrally concerned with the expression of human values in literature. They admire forthright moral heroism. Many are sensitive to traditional moral and philosophical backgrounds of literature. Critics so predisposed respond positively to Santiago's resolute struggle and to his spiritual transcendence of physical defeat. They approve Hemingway's tendency to the idealistic and visionary in his conception of Santiago's transcendence. Most of them praise Hemingway's vision of an orderly universe. (That *The Old Man and the Sea* can also be read at the level of the kindred *popular* American tradition of the self-reliant individual triumphing over adversity in an orderly moral universe—as in the Western—perhaps explains its unusual simultaneous success with the mass circulation audience of *Life* and with many scholarly critics.)

Dissenting critics, more skeptical, tend to believe in disorder (internal and external) as the essential condition of man's world.[17] They

[15] A number of those particularly hostile to *The Old Man and the Sea* are identified with the *Partisan Review* temper, approving literary experimentation and, in the 1960's, radical politics. The favorable critics do not have such a clear group identity, but several of them have shown interest in Romantic and Transcendental writers (Shelley and Emerson, for example).

[16] Note, for example, the terms of the context Cleanth Brooks establishes for discussing the works of Hemingway (including *The Old Man and the Sea*, in which Brooks says—*The Hidden God*, p. 14—"the dignity of man is asserted") and other modern authors. The terms would be alien to the critics who disparage *The Old Man and the Sea* (compare Note 17 below):

One looks [when he comes to estimate the achievement of the serious writers of our times] for an image of man, attempting in a world increasingly dehumanized to realize himself as a man—to act like a responsible moral being, not to drift like a mere thing.

The Hidden God: Studies in Hemingway, Faulkner, Yeats, Eliot, and Warren (New Haven: Yale University Press, 1963), p. 4.

[17] Compare Brooks, Note 16 above, with the introductory context Leslie Fiedler establishes for discussing some of the same authors and according to which he judges *The Old Man and the Sea* a failure (on p. 18, *No! in Thunder*):

The vision of the truly contemporary writer is that of a world not only absurd but also chaotic and fragmentary. . . . the contemporary American writer can abjure negativism only if he is willing to sacrifice truth and art. For major novelists and minor, the pursuit of the positive means stylistic suicide. Language itself decays, and dialogue becomes travesty; character, stereotype; insight, sentiment.

No! in Thunder, pp. 17–18.

see forms of order as tentative impositions, subject to revolutionary
change. From these premises derives their more intense concern than
that of humanist critics with literary form *per se*. They admire
novelists who call attention to their own artifice, directly or meta-
phorically, in order to indicate that art is the imposition of order
upon a disorderly world. They applaud radical literary experimentation and sometimes speak in the 1960's about the disintegration of the
novel form as a manifestation of disintegrating social order. They are
partisans of the anti-hero (variously the underground man or the
victim) upon whom forms and identity are pressed against his will.
Such critics would naturally have a greater temperamental affinity for
the early Hemingway fiction, in which the hero is the victim of circumstances not of his own making, in which ritual appears as man's
artifice for creating order, and spare, stylized prose a defense against
emotional disintegration, than for the emotionally secure heroism
and orderliness of *The Old Man and the Sea*. And most of them do in
fact praise the early Hemingway, using it as one standard by which
to disparage *The Old Man and the Sea*.

A disagreement based, as this one seems to be, on general philosophical and aesthetic principles is probably not resolvable by appeal to
the text of *The Old Man and the Sea*. Critics bring the same specific
details and the same general qualities of the story to bear in support
of "masterpiece" and in support of "fraud."

V

The Old Man and the Sea has been compared with many established
literary classics—from *The Odyssey* and Job to *Lord Jim* and "The
Bear." (That the comparisons which immediately suggest themselves
are almost exclusively with traditional classics rather than with works
contemporary with *The Old Man and the Sea* points to a tradition-
alism/modernism split as a further explanation of divided critical
opinion.) To an extent, the comparisons, which critics of both persua-
sions make in support of their arguments, are shaped by the same
tastes which determine critics' use of internal textual evidence, and
hence they tend to be as inconclusive in establishing a final judgment
about the literary merit of *The Old Man and the Sea*. Nevertheless it
is interesting to explore a few of the relationships which *The Old
Man and the Sea* has to established tradition—especially to its own
American tradition. One can at least *speculate* on the likelihood of its
survival as an important work on the basis of what comparison reveals about its kinship with tradition and about its distinctive qualities.

Among the important links between *The Old Man and the Sea*

and a number of American classics is its concentration on the struggle for survival of an individual set against the background of a community from which he is estranged. Like Natty Bumppo in the Leatherstocking novels, Thoreau at Walden, Huck Finn in his *Adventures,* Ike McCaslin in "The Bear," or Jake Barnes in *The Sun Also Rises,* Santiago is an outsider in some sense from his community. But Santiago's separation is not radical alienation. It derives from his being *salao,* unlucky, precisely with respect to the established values of his community; he has not caught any fish for eighty-four days. His bad luck jeopardizes a prized championship defined by communal values. His self-definition is not created in active opposition to society, nor is it threatened by society, as is the case with the other heroes named above. The skeletal evidence of Santiago's still formidable prowess as a fisherman restores community respect and reinforces the compassion which much of the community has felt for him all along.

That Santiago tests his championship and experiences his spiritual renewal away from the village in unspoiled nature again links *The Old Man and the Sea* to familiar tradition. Numerous American heroes escape to nature to preserve their sense of selfhood, their vital freedom. Natty Bumppo moves west ahead of the frontier; Thoreau immerses himself in Walden; Huck takes to his raft on the Mississippi; Jake Barnes goes fishing at Burguete. Santiago, whom Hemingway associates with the enduring vitality of the sea in the title and by the color of his cheerful and undefeated eyes (p. 10), clearly derives strength of body and character from his intimate relationship with the sea, his *"la mar."* And in so doing he stands, not alienated, but as a symbolic ideal for his community. (See Rovit, p. 105 below.) Only the young fishermen with motorboats who use the masculine form *"el mar"* and think the sea an enemy (pp. 29–30) are moving away from communal values rooted in nature and toward the civilized debility of the tourists who cannot tell marlins from sharks (pp. 126–27). These few hints of the corrupting effects of modern civilization are the only indication of the usually more fully developed conflict in American literature between timeless primal wisdom based on intimacy with nature and sophisticated knowledge involved with human institutions and historical change. Cooper, Thoreau, Twain, Faulkner, and Hemingway himself in his early fiction give serious intellectual and emotional recognition to the counterforces of civilization and history; Hemingway in *The Old Man and the Sea* comes close to unqualified celebration of primitive or childlike intimacy with nature as the means to spiritual transcendence.

At first glance, the sharks, Portuguese men-of-war, and potential hurricanes of Hemingway's sea might suggest that he shares the qualified view of nature held by dark American writers—that nature

in her duplicity offers perils along with vitality and freedom. But
Santiago's intimate at-homeness in nature—the great fish is "friend"
and "brother"; the stars are "distant friends"; even the dangerous
Portuguese man-of-war is, familiarly, " *'Agua mala'*. . . . 'You whore' "
—recalls Thoreau's intimacy (though not Thoreau's sophistication)
with the tame world of Walden more than Ishmael's uncertain relationship with the treacherous sea in Melville's *Moby Dick* or Goodman Brown's ambivalent attraction to the forest at night in Hawthorne's "Young Goodman Brown." There are no threats with
dark symbolic overtones in Santiago's nature. In the fiction of the
dark writers (and in the ancient folk tales from which it probably
derives—see Claire Rosenfield, pp. 41–42 below), the great beasts and
dark human adversaries which the hero confronts in the wilderness are
fearsome projections of the unknown, the dark, the violent, the
threatening, the evil. Melville's Negro in "Benito Cereno" and great
white whale in *Moby Dick* are of this tradition. So are Cooper's
Magua and his other bad Indians. And so, though his fearsomeness is
muted, is the bull in his ritual role in Hemingway's bullfighting
stories and *Death in the Afternoon*. But the beasts and adversary in
The Old Man and the Sea are not fearsome, directly or symbolically.
The physical punishment Santiago undergoes during his three days
at sea results directly from his resolution (resolution which comes to
him without intense inner struggle[18]) to hang on to the marlin rather
than cut loose. He is never represented as physically threatened by
the strength or malice of either marlin or sharks. If Santiago's
adversaries are understood as symbolic projections of his own qualities
(and all the noble opponents are identified with him in some way),
they confirm rather than call into question his resolute heroism. The
first beast opponent, the marlin, is himself a noble with a sword,
brother to the hero; the second, the mako shark, is kindred to the
hero's not very sinister left hand. The Negro handwrestling opponent,
for all the shadow he casts on the blue wall, proves, like the marlin,
a noble and worthy opponent. Any sense of danger and tension
is dispelled by the cozy familiarity with which human and animal
characters exchange flesh and blood in a kind of universal communion
—a peculiar blending of the themes of St. Francis and Jack London.

Somehow the serenely ordered *Old Man and the Sea*, with its
acceptance of the inevitability of natural rhythms, with its absence

[18] . . . a work of affirmation must contain its moment of despair—specifically,
there must be a bad moment when the old man Santiago is tempted to cut the
line and let the big fish go. Hemingway avoided the problem by never letting
the old man be seriously tempted. Like a giant (but not like a man) Santiago
just hung onto the fish. . . .

Norman Mailer, *Advertisements for Myself,* p. 19.

of psychological struggle in its hero, with its moral simplicity, in sum, pales when compared to the classics in American tradition, or in Western literary tradition at large, to which its action, theme, and literary techniques invite comparison. It gives the effect of action frozen in a graceful tableau for our moral and aesthetic contemplation—more in the manner of a medieval exemplum or Willa Cather's *Death Comes for the Archbishop* (enduring, but minor works) than of *King Lear* or *Moby Dick*. Or, if Lear and Ahab seem too tragically violent in their ends to offer fair comparison with Hemingway's Old Man, consider other old men who share Santiago's equanimity in the face of death—Oedipus in Sophocles' *Oedipus at Colonus* or Leatherstocking in Cooper's *The Prairie*. Oedipus moving to his mysterious translation and Leatherstocking sitting with his face to the west measure depths of complex individual and cultural experience which Santiago does not begin to reach with his weighted lines.

But if Hemingway's *The Old Man and the Sea* lacks the depth of an *Oedipus at Colonus,* its evoking such a comparison at all suggests that it merits the reader's serious attention. And, whether one sees it as fakery or as a parable of universal significance, the importance of Hemingway's last novel in his development is undeniable.

The Old Man and the Sea: Vision / Revision

by Philip Young

I

This book has many roots in the rest of Hemingway's work. Much of it goes back to an essay, "On the Blue Water (A Gulf Stream Letter)," which the author published in *Esquire,* in April of 1936. In this piece he tried to explain what there is about deep-sea fishing in the Stream that makes it exciting—the mysteries of that largely unexplored place, the indescribable strangeness, wildness, speed, power and beauty of the enormous marlin which inhabit it, and the struggle while their strength is bound to a man's, his thick line "taut as a banjo string and little drops coming from it." He also included a paragraph of more specific interest:

Another time an old man fishing alone in a skiff out of Cabañas hooked a great marlin that, on the heavy sashcord handline, pulled the skiff far out to sea. Two days later the old man was picked up by fishermen sixty miles to the eastward, the head and forward part of the marlin lashed alongside. What was left of this fish, less than half, weighed eight hundred pounds. The old man had stayed with him a day, a night, a day and another night while the fish swam deep and pulled the boat. When he had come up the old man had pulled the boat up on him and harpooned him. Lashed alongside the sharks had hit him and the old man had fought them out alone in the Gulf Stream in a skiff, clubbing them, stabbing at them, lunging at them with an oar until he was exhausted and the sharks had eaten all that they could hold. He was crying in the boat when the fishermen picked

---

"The Old Man and the Sea: *Vision/Revision*" [*Author's title for this reprinting*] *by Philip Young. I from Chapter 3, "Death and Transfiguration," and II from the "Afterword" of Ernest Hemingway: A Reconsideration (University Park: The Pennsylvania State University Press, 1966), pp. 123–33, 274–75. Copyright ©️ 1966 by Philip Young. Reprinted by permission of Philip Young.*

I repeats the author's 1952 reaction to The Old Man and the Sea; *II is his 1966 reconsideration.*

him up, half crazy from his loss, and the sharks were still circling the boat.

Here, of course, is the germ of the novel.[1] And the old man himself, Santiago, is also an outgrowth of past performances. Just as Col. Cantwell presented the Hemingway hero aged for the first time beyond his young manhood, so Santiago is the first of the code heroes to have grown old. Particularly he is related to men like Jack, the prizefighter, and Manuel Garcia, "The Undefeated" bullfighter, who lose in one way but win in another. Like Manuel, Santiago is a fighter whose best days are behind him, who is too old for what his profession demands of him and, worse, is wholly down on his luck. But he still dares, and sticks to the rules, and will not quit when he is licked. He is undefeated, he endures, and his loss therefore, in the manner of it, is itself a victory.

"A man can be destroyed but not defeated," is how Hemingway put it this time. And so the theme—"What a man can do and what a man endures" ("plenty," as Santiago admits of his suffering)—is also familiar. So are other things—Hemingway's concern with fishing as a deeply meaningful occupation, for instance, and his awareness of death, expertly delivered and received, as the source of much of life's

---

[1] On October 21, 1965, one Anselmo Hernandez, a gnarled, weathered old man allegedly 92 years old, made it to Key West, Florida, in the midst of thousands of anonymous refugees from the Castro regime. He became conspicuous, however, by announcing that he had "inspired" Hemingway's Nobel Prize-winning *The Old Man and the Sea:* "I knew Hemingway for thirty years. . . . He said he would write a novel about me and he did." This claim, widely printed in the press with a current photograph of the old fisherman, was immediately dismissed by Mrs. Hemingway, who commented that a dozen Cuban fishermen made the same boast further that although her husband had known Hernandez well the book was not based on any one person. Her statement was accepted as authoritative. But on seeing the photograph of Anselmo Hernandez, and seeming to recall both the image and the name in connection with the novel, the present writer dug up another picture (published by *Vogue* in June of 1953), and disputed Mrs. Hemingway on two counts. This earlier photograph was taken by Leland Heyward, producer of the film based on the book, and it shows a threesome seated in a bar "on location,"—purportedly the author of the story, Ernest Hemingway, together with the actor who was to play the old man, Spencer Tracy, and with the old man himself, who was identified only as "Anselmo." The Anselmo Hernandez whose picture was in the newspapers of October 22, 1965, is older and thinner and unmistakably the Anselmo of the 1953 photograph. Surely the character of Hemingway's old man is no transcript of any Anselmo's; it is chiefly the character of the author-fisherman himself. But if the experience of the old man in the book is not based on exactly what happened to an actual, single fisherman then Hemingway in 1936 gratuitously invented what he pretended in *Esquire* to report. And if Hernandez is not the same old man then Hemingway was party to a second deception when he sat for Heyward's photograph. Neither deceit is probable: Hemingway had a fondness for facts as well as fictions.

intensity. In a way we have even known the boy before, for in providing that sentimental adulation which in his need for love and pity
the other hero once required, Manolin has taken over some of the
functions hitherto performed by the heroine.

There is little that is new, either, in the technique. The action is
swift, tight, exact; the construction is perfect, and the story is exciting. There is the same old zest for the right details. And there is
the extraordinary vividness of the background—the sea, which is
very personal to Santiago, whose knowledge of it, and feeling for it,
bring it brilliantly and lovingly close. Again there is the foreign
speech translated—realistic, fresh and poetic all at once. In short,
The Old Man and the Sea, in manner and meaning, is unmistakable
Hemingway. But where characteristic methods and attitudes have
on rare occasion failed him in the past, or have been only partly
successful, this short novel is beyond any question a triumph.

This is the first time, in all of Hemingway's work, that the code
hero and the Hemingway hero have not been wholly distinct. Wilson
the guide, Cayetano the gambler, Morgan the smuggler—all embodied ideals of behavior the Hemingway hero could not sustain.
They balanced his deficiencies; they corrected his stance. Of course
Santiago is not Hemingway, and is not the Hemingway hero; he is
the code hero, based on the experience of an unfictional Cuban fisherman. But now the relation of the author and the code hero is very
close. Though Hemingway was thought with the phrase to be acknowl-
edging his eccentricity, whereas Santiago makes it clear that he means
he is formidable, both figures were given to remarking "I am a
strange old man." And both men were preoccupied with their "luck"
—a kind of magic which people have in them, or do not. Indeed it is
the only flaw in the book, beyond our involuntary recollections of
the heroine, that there are times when the old fisherman sounds a
little like Col. Cantwell: "Do not think about sin," Santiago tells
himself with uncharacteristic sarcasm. "There are people who are
paid to do it."

What this means, among other things, is that Hemingway was
narrowing the gap that had always existed between him and his
code heroes. Actually he narrowed it to the point where it is possible
to show that on one level *The Old Man and the Sea* was wholly
personal: as he seemed obscurely to acknowledge his demotion in
Across the River by removing the stars from Cantwell's shoulders, so
here Hemingway seemed, but more obviously, to promote himself
back. Harry, dying in "The Snows of Kilimanjaro," was himself a
writer, and the Hemingway hero, but not even that story contained
a more transparent or confident discussion by the author of those
constantly absorbing problems of his professional past, present and

future. *The Old Man and the Sea* is, from one angle, an account of Hemingway's personal struggle, grim, resolute and eternal, to write his best. With his seriousness, his precision and his perfectionism, Hemingway saw his craft exactly as Santiago sees his. The fishing and the fishermen turn out to be metaphors so apt that they need almost no translation: Santiago is a master who sets his lines with more care than his colleagues, but he has no luck any more. It would be better to be lucky, he thinks, but he will be skillfully exact instead; then when the luck comes he will be ready for it. Once he was very strong. "The Champion" they called him, and he had beaten many rivals in fair fights. The boy agrees: "There are many good fishermen and some great ones. But there is only you." Still there are many who do not know this, and the whole reputation is gravely imperilled by a streak of bad luck. And so the ex-champion musters his confidence: "I may not be as strong as I think. . . . But I know many tricks and I have resolution."

Santiago needs these things, for he is still out for the really big fish. He has assured the boy he is a strange old man; "Now is when I must prove it." (The times that he has proved it before "meant nothing. Now he was proving it again.") And he does prove it. The sharks may eat his fish, and spoil everything, as they always try to do. But even a young fisherman in the prime of his strength would have done well to land this marlin, and so at the end Santiago is secure in bed, dreaming happily of the lions. (As for these lions, they play like cats on beaches "so white they hurt your eyes"—as white, we might think, as the "unbelievably white" top of Kilimanjaro that Harry dreamed of, the magical goal of the artist, where the leopard froze. And so we could say here, as Hemingway said of Harry, that Santiago is happy in the end because he knows that "there was where he was going.")

But this time it is the public and not the private parable—the generalized meanings which underlie and impregnate the action—that matters most. On this level there is no allegory in the book and, strictly speaking, no symbols. The marlin Santiago catches, the sharks that eat it away and the lions he dreams of are not so much symbolic of other things as broadly suggestive of them. To pin them down by naming equivalents they do not have would be to limit and decrease, vulgarly and gratuitously, the power of what Hemingway had written. On the public level the lions, for instance, are only so vague as the "poetry" in Santiago, and perhaps the sign of his nostalgia for his youth. The marlin is not even anything so general as "nature"—which would justify the most obvious trap, a man-vs.-nature allegory—for as brothers in this world and life, inextricably joined by the necessity of killing and being killed, Santiago and the

fish are tightly bound up in the same thing. If we ask ourselves what
The Old Man and the Sea is "about" on a public and figurative level,
we can only answer "life," which is the finest and most ambitious
thing for a parable to be about. Hemingway has written about life:
a struggle against the impossible odds of unconquerable natural forces
in which—given such a fact as that of death—a man can only lose, but
which he can dominate in such a way that his loss has dignity, itself
the victory.

The stories of all the best parables are sufficient to themselves, and
many will prefer to leave the meanings of this one unverbalized.
Such a reading, however, would comprehend less than Hemingway
clearly intended. By stripping his book—as only this novelist can—
of all but the essentials, and Santiago himself of all but the last
things he needs for his survival (the old man owns almost nothing,
and hardly even eats), and by the simplicity of the characterization and
the style, Hemingway has gently but powerfully urged a metaphor
which stands for what life can be. And it is an epic metaphor, a
contest where even the problem of moral right and wrong seems
paltry if not irrelevant—as in ancient epics, exactly—before the
great thing that is this struggle.

If all this sounds a little "classical," it is because this tale of courage,
endurance, pride, humility and death is remarkably so. It is classical
not only technically, in its narrow confines, its reduction to funda-
mentals, the purity of its design, and even in the fatal flaw of pride
(for Santiago exceeded his limits and went out too far). It is also
classical in spirit, in its mature acceptance, and even praise, of
things as they are. It is much in the spirit of the Greek tragedies
in which men fight against great odds and win moral victories, losing
only such tangible rewards—however desirable the prizes and heartbreaking the losses—as will dissipate anyway. It is especially like
Greek tragedy in that as the hero fails and falls, one gets an unfor-
gettable glimpse of what stature a man may have.

The story has affiliations, too, with Christian lore. These are not
so much this time in its spirit, despite the virtues of pity, humility and
charity with which it is invested. They are in its several allusions
to Christian symbolism, particularly of the crucifixion. This orienta-
tion was not entirely new to Hemingway. Nearly forty years ago he
published a little play, "Today Is Friday," in which a Roman soldier
who was present at Calvary kept saying of Jesus: "He was pretty
good in there today." In *Across the River and Into the Trees* the
Colonel, whose heart goes out to anyone who has been hit hard,
"as every man will be if he stays," has a twice-wounded and misshapen
hand, which he is very conscious of. Renata, running her fingers

lightly over the scars, tells him she has strangely dreamed it is "the hand of Our Lord." Now it is Santiago's hands, and the noise that comes from him when he sees the sharks ("a noise such as a man might make, involuntarily, feeling the nail go through his hands and into the wood"), which first relate his ordeal to an ancient one. Then when at the end he carries his mast uphill to his cabin, and falls, exhausted, but finally makes it, and collapses on his cot, "face down . . . with his arms out straight and the palms of his hands up," the allusion is unmistakable.

All this does not indicate that Hemingway was embracing, or even necessarily approaching, the Christian faith. Such passages as the one on the possible nonexistence of sin explicitly disavow it, as does the running insistence on the story as a wholly natural parable, confined to the realms of this world and what we know by experience. Instead Hemingway is implying another metaphor, and seems to say here, as in *Across the River:* the world not only breaks, it crucifies, everyone, and afterwards many are scarred in the hands. But now he has gone further, to add that when it comes, and they nail you up, the important thing is to be pretty good in there like Santiago.

One of the virtues of this short novel is that its meanings emerge from the action with all the self-contained power of the marlin breaking the surface of the ocean. Hemingway did not drag up anything, and one of the means whereby he kept the parable from obtruding is the baseball—that force in Santiago's life which, beside the lions, is all the life he has beyond his calling. Baseball stars are the heroes of this simple man; their exploits are the incidents, and their pennant races the plots, of his mythology. Baseball works a charm on the pages of this book. The talk about it is vastly real, it gives a little play to the line when unrelieved tension would be dangerous, and the sober conversations about it, which Santiago conducts with himself and with the boy, are delicious in their own right:

> "The Yankees cannot lose."
> "But I fear the Indians of Cleveland."
> "Have faith in the Yankees my son. Think of the great DiMaggio."
> "I fear both the Tigers of Detroit and the Indians of Cleveland."
> "Be careful or you will fear even the Reds of Cincinnati and the White Sox of Chicago."

Nowhere in the book is there the slightest touch of condescension in the humor of this childlike preoccupation. Hemingway gave it without irony, without patronizing his characters, without unkindness. This is because he profoundly respected his characters, and wrote his book with a tenderness that was new to him and to his work. And that is an important perception, because it leads to the heart of the book's power.

"I love more than any son of the great bitch alive," said the Colonel in *Across the River,* and although he said it "not aloud" it sounded foolish anyway. But it sounds a little less silly now: *The Old Man and the Sea* is a powerful book, and a large part of its power is the power of love.

Santiago's respect for his foe, the marlin, which is love, actually, as for a brother, is surpassed by Hemingway's respect for both that fish and Santiago himself, and for the whole of life which this battle epitomizes, and the world that contains it. An extraordinary thing had happened, for somehow or other a reverence for life's struggle, which this contest dramatizes, and for mankind, for which Santiago stands as a possibility, had descended on Hemingway like the gift of grace on the religious. This veneration for humanity, for what can be done and endured, and this grasp of man's kinship with the other creatures of the world, and with the world itself, is itself a victory of substantial proportions. It is the knowledge that a simple man is capable of such decency, dignity, and even heroism, and that his struggle can be seen in heroic terms, that largely distinguishes this book. For the knowledge that a man can be great, and his life great, might be in itself an approach to greatness. To have had the skill, then, to convince others that this is a valid vision is Hemingway's achievement.

This is to say, among other less abstract things, that Hemingway had reached the point where he was able to affirm without forcing, or even apparent effort, certain things about brotherhood, man, and life which he had tried and crucially failed to affirm in *For Whom the Bell Tolls.* Indeed, since Santiago is a man alone and without the boy—for, after all, a man faces certain final things alone—and since the old man catches his fish, Hemingway had sharply qualified the pronouncement of *To Have and Have Not,* which was even more forced. *The Old Man and the Sea* is pregnant with implications about the contestants and the contest, but this time there is no need to say anything about them outright. It seems you never have to say it if you really mean it.

It is the heartening vision of this story, then, and the deep sense one has of a writer who is at long last completely at home in this life and world, which chiefly account for the power of the book. The rest of its force is the result of its remarkable surface virtues. And it may be that the action—so taut that beads of water seem to jump off the lines, all in a world miraculously alive and lasting—will seem one day the greatest thing after all. Hemingway's hope for his short novel, that "all the things that are in it do not show, but only are with you after you have read it," is mostly fulfilled; and, in the end, vicarious experience is the finest gift literature has to offer. It is the genius of Hemingway that our response is intense, rich, and deep. Without that, the vision and the meanings would count for nothing.

"It's as though I had gotten finally what I had been working for all my life," Hemingway also said, and there are many ways in which it would seem that he had. One of the more subtle ways lies in the fact of Santiago's survival: all the rest of the characters Hemingway projected himself deeply into have, if they struggled and attained the code, died in the process; at the end of this story Santiago is confident, happy, and ready for more. In addition, though *The Old Man and the Sea* is not necessarily Hemingway's greatest book, it is the one in which he said the finest single thing he ever had to say as well as he could ever hope to say it.

And so the question occurred to the faithless: then what was left for this one to do? To ask such a question was to reckon without the personal triumph Santiago represented and to forget what the old man said when the boy asked if he was strong enough then for a truly big fish: "I think so. And there are many tricks." Besides, this was indeed a strange old man.

II

If one were rewriting instead of revising this book, one thing he would greatly tone down is his praise for *The Old Man and the Sea,* with which he went farther out than Santiago.[2] (One critic, Marvin Mudrick, wrote recently that I treated it as if it were one of Beethoven's last quartettes.) The feeling is now that although the tale is here and there exciting it is itself drawn out a little far. Even the title seems an affectation of simplicity, and the realization that Hemingway was now trading on and no longer inventing the style that made him famous came just too late. Redolent of self-admiration, Manolin's boyish worship of the old man is harder than ever to take. The boy himself once seemed a "substitute heroine," but the book by brother Leicester Hemingway supplied a better insight:

> Ernest was never very content with life unless he had a spiritual kid brother nearby . . . someone he could show off to as well as teach. He needed uncritical admiration. . . . A little worshipful awe was a distinct aid. . . . I made a good kid brother when I was around.

[2] [Professor Young has revised the first sentence of this passage for this reprinting.—Ed. note.]

Heroine or kid brother, this need was almost always part of the trouble when Hemingway was around in the novels; self-praise is always most embarrassing. And, this time, identifying with his "code hero" brought on confusion as well. Thick as a "pencil," and set out with more care than the opposition's, Hemingway was thinking more of his own lines than Santiago's; allegory overwhelms reality when we are told that the young boy carries this fishing line—three-quarters of a mile of it—plus a harpoon and the gaff to the boat. (A gaffe indeed, unless, as we are not told, the lad was actually a giant.) Similarly it does not make very much sense to say that *Santiago* "went out too far": he did after all boat his fish out there, and the sharks that took it away from him are not confined to waters distant from land. It is not so much that Santiago was a fisherman in whom the writer saw himself; rather that Hemingway was a writer who thought he could disguise himself as Santiago. The autobiographical element unfortunately triumphs again: it wasn't Into the Caribbean but *Across the River* where somebody felt he went out too far. Hemingway, taking a view of that failed novel which occasionally overrode his concern for his sea story, went way out and hooked his great prize, a book to keep a man all winter, but then the critics ate away at it until there was nothing left. Not as strong as he had been once, he felt that he was still the master of many tricks and still up to bringing in the big one—which, in his opinion, may have been the same small book that was the allegory of his vicissitudes.

The Boy and the Lions

by Carlos Baker

The relationship between Santiago and the boy Manolo is of a special and memorable kind. In the light of the experiment in symbolic doubling which Hemingway tried in *Across The River and Into The Trees,* the meaning of this other relationship becomes clear. In one of her aspects, Renata stands for Colonel Cantwell's lost youth. Manolo fulfills a similar purpose, and with greater success in that we do not have to overcome the doubt raised by the difference of sexes between the Colonel and his lady. To claim such a purpose for Manolo is not, of course, to discount his dramatic function, which is to heighten our sympathy with the old fisherman. At the beginning and end of the story, we watch Santiago through the boy's admiring and pitying eyes. From the charitable . . . Martin, owner of The Terrace, Manolo brings Santiago a last supper of black beans and rice, fried bananas, stew, and two bottles of beer. On the morning of the expedition, Manolo arranges for the simple breakfast of coffee in condensed milk cans. He also procures the albacores and sardines which Santiago will use for bait. After helping to launch the skiff, the boy sees Santiago off in the dark with a wish for his luck on this eighty-fifth day. At the close of the story, after the ordeal, Manolo brings coffee and food for the old man's waking, and ointment for his injured hands, commiserating on the loss, and planning for a future when they will work side by side again. The love of Manolo for Santiago is that of a disciple for a master in the arts of fishing.[1] It is also the love of a son for an adopted father.

"The Boy and the Lions" by Carlos Baker. Section III of Chapter XII, "The Ancient Mariner," from Hemingway: The Writer as Artist, *3rd ed. (Princeton: Princeton University Press, 1963), pp. 304–11. Copyright 1952, 1956, © 1963 by Carlos Baker. Reprinted by permission of Princeton University Press and the author.*

[1] The disciple-master relationship is established early with a playing upon the words *doubt* and *faith.* See the colloquy between man and boy, *The Old Man and the Sea,* The Scribner Library (New York: Charles Scribner's Sons, 1952), pp. 10–11.

But from Santiago's point of view the relationship runs deeper. He has known the boy for years, from the period of childhood up to this later time when Manolo stands, strong and lucky and confident, on the edge of young manhood. Like many other aging men, Santiago finds something reassuring about the overlay of the past upon the present. Through the agency of Manolo he is able to recapture in his imagination, and therefore to a certain degree in fact, the same strength and confidence which distinguished his own young manhood as a fisherman, earning him the title of *El Campéon*.[2]

During the old man's ordeal, the two phrases, "I wish the boy was here," and "I wish I had the boy," play across Santiago's mind often enough to merit special attention. In each instance he means exactly what he says: the presence of the boy would be a help in a time of crisis. But he is also invoking by means of these phrases the strength and courage of his youth. Soon after he has hooked his marlin and knows that he must hang onto the line for some time, Santiago says, "I wish I had the boy." Immediately his resolution tightens. During the first night he says it again. He is just reflecting that "no one should be alone in their old age," though in this case it is unavoidable. Again, and as if the mere mention of the boy were a kind of talisman, he then resolves to eat the tuna he has caught, though the thought of the raw fish sickens him, "in order to keep strong." Later the same night, he says aloud, "I wish the boy was here"—and promptly settles himself against the planks of the bow for another period of endurance. Near dawn he says again, "I wish I had the boy." Then he upbraids himself for wishful thinking. "But you haven't got the boy, he thought. You have only yourself and you had better work back to the last line now . . . and cut it away and hook up the two reserve coils." So he does exactly that.

As he summons the courage to eat the raw tuna for his breakfast on the second day, he links the boy and salt in what amounts to a metaphor: "I wish the boy were here and that I had some salt." Then he proves to himself that he has enough of both in their metaphorical meaning to eat the tuna and renew his waning strength. While he wills to unknot the cramp, he thinks that "if the boy was here" a little massaging would loosen the muscles of

---

[2] Santiago uses two other images to give himself confidence during the ordeal. One is the great DiMaggio of the New York Yankees, himself the son of a fisherman, and just then suffering from a bonespur in his heel. The old man gains strength from the idea of DiMaggio's performing with a champion's grace despite the pressure of his affliction. See esp. pp. 68 and 103–4. Santiago's second image is of himself in his prime, handwrestling with the great negro dockworker from Cienfuegos. See pp. 68–70. But it is to the image of the boy that the old man returns most often.

the forearm and maybe help the still useless gnarled claw of the hand. Yet when, soon afterwards, his great marlin breaches, Santiago summons the strength he needs to play his fish.

On the next breaching it is the same. While the marlin leaps again and again, unseen in the darkness of the second night, and while the old man and his line are both strained and stretched almost to the breaking-point, he triples the refrain: "If the boy was here he would wet the coils of line . . . Yes. If the boy were here. If the boy were here." Once more the effect of the invocation is nearly magical as if, by means of it, some of the strength of youth flowed in to sustain the limited powers of age. Always, just after he has said the words, Santiago manages to reach down into the well of his courage for one more dipperful. Then he goes on.

From this point onwards, having served its purpose, the refrain vanishes. It is not until the return voyage, while the old man reflects Job-like on the problem of the connection between sin and suffering and while the sharks collect their squadrons unseen in the dark waters, that the boy's image returns again. "Everything kills everything else in some way," he tells himself. "Fishing kills me exactly as it keeps me alive." Then he corrects the misapprehensions that can come from false philosophizing. "The boy keeps me alive . . . I must not deceive myself too much." It is good, at this point, that the old man has the thought of the boy to keep him alive. For the sharks wait, and a very bad time is just ahead.[3]

In the night in which he is preparing for betrayal by the sharks, though he does not yet absolutely know that they will come, Santiago has recourse to yet another sustaining image—a pride of lions he once saw at play on an African beach when he was a young man like Manolo. Hemingway early establishes a clear symbolic connection between the boy and the lions. "When I was your age," Santiago says, "I was before the mast on a square rigged ship that ran to Africa and I have seen lions on the beaches in the evening." Manolo's answer—"I know. You told me."—indicates not only that the reminiscence has arisen before in their conversations, but also that the incident of the lions is a pleasant obsession in Santiago's mind. "There is for every man," writes the poet Yeats, "some one scene, some one adventure, some one picture that is the image of his secret life, and this one image, if he would but brood over it his life long, would lead his soul." Santiago finds such an image in the lions of his youthful experience.

The night before his ordeal, after the boy has left him to sleep, the old man dreams of the lions. "He was asleep in a short time

---

[3] For allusions to the boy, see esp. pp. 45, 48, 50, 51–52, 56, 62, 106.

and he dreamed of Africa when he was a boy and the long golden beaches and the white beaches, so white they hurt your eyes, and the high capes and the great brown mountains. He lived along that coast now every night and in his dreams he heard the surf roar and saw the native boats come riding through it. He smelled the tar and oakum of the deck as he slept and he smelled the smell of Africa that the land breeze brought at morning. Usually when he smelled the land breeze he woke up and dressed to go and wake the boy. But tonight the smell of the land breeze came very early and he knew it was too early in his dream and went on dreaming to see the white peaks of the Islands rising from the sea and then he dreamed of the different harbours and roadsteads of the Canary Islands."

Santiago "no longer dreamed of storms, nor of women, nor of great occurrences, nor of great fish, nor fights, nor contests of strength, nor of his wife. He only dreamed of places now and of the lions on the beach. They played like young cats in the dusk and he loved them as he loved the boy."

Early in the afternoon of his second day out, having strengthened his resolution by the saying of the prayers, Santiago thinks again about his lions. The marlin is pulling steadily. "I wish he'd sleep and I could sleep and dream about the lions," thinks Santiago. "Why are the lions the main thing that is left?" Much later the same day, "cramping himself against the line with all his body," and "putting all his weight onto his right hand," the old man manages to sleep. Soon then he begins to dream of the long yellow beach, and in the dream, we are told, "he saw the first of the lions come down onto it in the early dark and then the other lions came and he rested his chin on the wood of the bows where the ship lay anchored with the evening off-shore breeze and he waited to see if there would be more lions and he was happy." In his old age and the time of his suffering, Santiago is supported by the memory of his youth and the strength of his youth. Living so, in the past, he is happy. But there is the further realization that "the child is father to the man." Luckily for this old man, he has also the thought of the strength of the boy Manolo, a young lion of just the age Santiago was when he first sailed to Africa. These together help him to endure.[4]

They help in a very notable way. For the boy and the lions are related to one of the fundamental psychological laws of Santiago's —and indeed of human—nature. This is the constant wave-like operation of bracing and relaxation. The boy braces, the lions relax, as in the systolic-diastolic movement of the human heart. The phe-

[4] For allusions to the lions, see pp. 22, 25, 66, 81, 127.

nomenon is related to the alternation of sleep and waking through the whole range of physical nature. But it is also a law which fulfills itself on the level of mentality. Its effects can be traced in our reaction to works of literature like this story of the acquisition and loss of the great marlin. The basic rhythms of the novel, in its maritime sections, are essentially those of the groundswell of the sea. Again and again as the action unfolds, the reader may find that he is gradually brought up to a degree of quiet tension which he is barely able to accept, as in the ascent by a small craft of a slow enormous wave. When he has reached the theoretical peak of his resistance, the crest passes and he suddenly relaxes into a trough of rest. The rhythm of the story appears to be built on such a stress-yield, brace-relax alternation. The impression is furthered by the constant tension which Santiago and his fish maintain on the line which joins them. Again and again one finds the old man telling himself that he has stretched the cord to a degree just short of the breaking-point. Then the stress relaxes, and the involved reader relaxes with it. This prolonged tug-of-war involves not only the fisherman and his fish but also the reader and his own emotions.

The planned contiguity of the old man with the double image of the boy and the lions converts the story of Santiago, in one of its meanings, into a parable of youth and age. It may be suggested that Hemingway, who read the whole of Conrad during the days of his writing apprenticeship in Paris and Toronto, has recollected the central strategy of Conrad's long short story, "Youth." For that story is built upon a brilliant contrast between young and old manhood. The ill-fated voyage of the barque *Judea,* out of London bound for Bangkok, shows young Marlow, with all the illusions and prowess of his youth, working side by side with old Captain Beard, the ship's master and a brave man. "He was sixty, if a day," says Marlow of the captain. "And he had blue eyes in that old face of his, which were amazingly like a boy's, with that candid expression some quite common men preserve to the end of their days by a rare internal gift of simplicity of heart and rectitude of soul." Again Marlow says, as the fated ship beats her way through a sea of trouble, that Beard was "immense in the singleness of his idea."

It may of course be a coincidence that these are qualities which Santiago shares. If so, it is a happy one. Two "quite common men" rise to the level of the heroic through simplicity of heart, rectitude of soul, and that immensity which is gained for them through the singleness of their concentration on a particular object. "Do or die" is the motto which adorns in flaking gilt the stern-timbers of the old *Judea.* The same words might with equal justice be carved into the weather-beaten wood of Santiago's skiff.

Conrad's story depends for its effect not only upon the contrast between young Marlow and old Beard but also, since the story is told some twenty years after the event, upon the contrast between the aging Marlow and his remembrance of his own youthful self. Santiago happily recalls the lions on the shore of Africa. Marlow recollects the brown men on the jetty of a Javanese port. This was where the small boats from the wrecked *Judea,* filled with exhausted men, at last reached the land. "I remember my youth," says Marlow, "and the feeling that will never come back any more—the feeling that I could last for ever, outlast the sea, the earth, and all men; the deceitful feeling that lures us on to joys, to perils, to love, to vain effort—to death; the triumphant conviction of strength, the heat of life in the handful of dust, the glow in the heart that with every year grows dim, grows cold, grows small, and expires." This feeling, which William Hazlitt has well described as the feeling of immortality in youth, is closely associated in Marlow's mind with the East—"the mysterious shores, the still water, the lands of the brown nations." As he tells his auditors: "For me, all the East is contained in that vision of my youth. It is all in that moment when I opened my young eyes on it. I came upon it from a tussle with the sea—and I was young—and I saw it looking at me. And this is all that is left of it! Only a moment; a moment of strength, of romance, of glamour— of youth!"

For Santiago it is not the coast of Java but that of Africa, not the faces of the brown men crowding the jetty but the playing lions, which carry the associations of youth, strength, and even immortality. "This is all that is left of it," cries Marlow of his youthful vision. "Why are the lions the main thing that is left?" cries Hemingway's old man in the midst of his ordeal. For both of them, in Marlow's words, it is "the time to remember." Santiago manages to put his vision to work in the great trial of his old age. "I told the boy I was a strange old man," he says. "Now is when I must prove it." And the author adds: "The thousand times that he had proved it meant nothing. Now he was proving it again. Each time was a new time and he never thought about the past when he was doing it." If he does not, at such times, think about the past to brood over it, he periodically calls back what it means to him through the double vision of the boy and the lions. If he can prove his mettle for the thousand-and-first time, there is no reason short of death why he cannot continue to prove it, as long as his vision lasts.

Of how many events in the course of human life may this not be said? It is Marlow once more who reminds us of the way in which one account of one man on one journey can extend outwards in our imaginations until it easily becomes a paradigm of the course of all men's lives. "You fellows know," says Marlow, beginning his account of the *Judea*, "there are those voyages that seem ordered for the illustration of life, that might stand for a symbol of existence. You fight, work, sweat, nearly kill yourself, sometimes do kill yourself, trying to accomplish something—and you can't. Not from any fault of yours." If it is so with the *Judea*, bound for Bangkok, do or die, it is so with Santiago of Havana, bound for home, with the sharks just beginning to smell the blood of his great fish. Do or die. In such works as these we all put to sea. Santiago makes his voyage on what used to be known as the Spanish Main. But it is also, by the process of synecdoche, that more extensive main, or mainstream, where we all drift or sail, with or against the wind, in fair weather or foul, with our prize catches and our predatory sharks, and each of us, perhaps, like the ancient mariner of Coleridge, with some kind of albatross hanging round his neck.

Fakery in *The Old Man and the Sea*

by *Robert P. Weeks*

I

From the vignettes and stories of his first book, *In Our Time,* to his last, *The Old Man and the Sea,* Ernest Hemingway repeatedly made skillful use of animals to epitomize the subjective state or the situation of his characters. Nick Adams' trout holding itself steady against the cold current of the Big Two-Hearted River, Francis Macomber's gut-shot lion standing off death in the tall grass, the huge, filthy vultures keeping a death-watch on Harry on the plains at the foot of Kilimanjaro—objectively and precisely epitomize the crisis confronting the protagonist in each of these stories.

Yet these animals, and the others Hemingway uses to perform the same function, are nonetheless marvelously real. They possess in abundance what James called solidity of specification: they move, sound, and look like real animals.

The difference, however, in the effectiveness with which Hemingway employs this characteristic device in his best work and in *The Old Man and the Sea* is illuminating. The work of fiction in which Hemingway devoted the most attention to natural objects, *The Old Man and the Sea,* is pieced out with an extraordinary quantity of fakery, extraordinary because one would expect to find no inexactness, no romanticizing of natural objects in a writer who loathed W. H. Hudson, could not read Thoreau, deplored Melville's rhetoric in *Moby Dick,* and who was himself criticized by other writers, notably Faulkner, for his devotion to the facts and his unwillingness to "invent."

Santiago, the only human being in the story, is himself depicted as a natural phenomenon, a strange old man whose heart beats like a turtle's, whose "feet and hands are like theirs," whose eyes are "the

"Fakery in The Old Man and the Sea*" by Robert P. Weeks. From* College English, *XXIV (December, 1962), 188–92. Copyright © 1962 by the National Council of Teachers of English. Reprinted by permission of the National Council of Teachers of English and Robert P. Weeks.*

same color as the sea" and with which he could once "see quite well in the dark. Not in the absolute dark. But almost as a cat sees." But even these natural affinities do not prepare us for what this strange old man can do. As he sits in his skiff with more than six hundred feet of heavy line—the thickness of a pencil—slanting steeply down into the darkness of the stream, Santiago feels a fish nibble at the bait.

> He felt no strain nor weight and he held the line lightly. Then it came again. This time it was a tentative pull, not solid nor heavy, and he knew exactly what it was. One hundred fathoms down a marlin was eating the sardines that covered the point and the shank of the hook where the hand-forged hook projected from the head of the small tuna.

This is not fishing skill; it's clairvoyance. The signals that can be transmitted over a pencil-thick line dangling more than six hundred feet into the ocean are relatively gross. Moreover, as Hemingway himself points out in his essay "Marlin Off Cuba," in *American Big Game Fishing,* published in an elegant limited edition of 906 copies by the Derrydale Press in 1935, one cannot tell whether the fish taking his bait is a marlin or a broadbill for they "take the bait in much the same manner, first, perhaps picking off a few of the sardines with which the point of the hook is covered, then seizing the whole fish used as bait between their jaws to crush it a moment before swallowing it."

This hint that Hemingway may be padding his characterization of Santiago by means of fakery is abundantly confirmed by the action that follows. His combat with the fish is an ordeal that would do in even a vigorous young man. He is at sea nearly three full days, almost all of that time without sleep and during much of it hanging onto a 1,500 pound fish that steadily tows him and his boat for miles, most of it *against* the current of the Gulf Stream. At noon on the third day, the giant fish circles the boat and the old man harpoons it, lashes it to the boat, and sets sail for home. Almost at once the sharks attack the fish, and the old man attacks the sharks. He battles them for more than twelve hours, quitting only when he runs out of weapons. Then, competently—and evidently without sleeping—he sails his little skiff for his home port, arriving shortly before dawn.

The extent to which this is an incredible performance is made clear when we turn to Hemingway himself for some notion of how an actual old Cuban fisherman behaved under similar circumstances. In "On the Blue Water," an essay that appeared in *Esquire* in 1936, Hemingway described how an old Cuban fisherman out in the Atlantic alone had been towed sixty miles to sea by a large marlin. When he was picked up by fishermen two days later with the marlin lashed to his small boat, the old man was weeping, half-demented, and sharks circled his boat.

It is hardly surprising that Santiago's clairvoyancy also enables him to be an uncanny meteorologist. While he is being towed by his fish, he looks at the sky, then soliloquizes: "If there is a hurricane you always see the signs of it in the sky for days ahead, if you are at sea. They do not see it ashore because they do not know what to look for." Scientists on land, sea, and in the air equipped with delicate pressure-sensing devices and radar cannot duplicate the powers that Hemingway off-handedly—and unconvincingly—gives to Santiago. According to the Chief District Meteorologist of the United States Weather Bureau in Miami, Florida, Gordon E. Dunn, "It is usually impossible to see signs of a tropical storm for more than two days in advance and on occasion it is difficult to tell for sure that there is a tropical storm in the vicinity for even a day in advance."

But it is when Santiago's fish makes its first appearance that the fakery truly begins to flow. For example, the old man perceives at once that it is a male. Hemingway heroes almost always measure themselves against male animals, whether they are kudu, lions, bear, bulls, or fish. The tragedy enacted in the bull ring becomes a farce if you replace the bull with a cow. The hunter, the torero, the fisherman prove that *they* have *cojones* by engaging another creature that has them beyond dispute. Santiago's marlin is both huge and possessed of incredible endurance. He tows man and boat for nearly three days.

But the marlin presents problems. Its *cojones* are internal. "The sexes are not recognizable in these animals except by internal dissection," according to Gilbert Voss, an icthyologist with the University of Miami Marine Laboratory. Confronted by this dilemma—by the need to pit his hero against a male fish on the one hand, but a fish whose sex he won't be able to determine by dissection before the sharks devour all the evidence, on the other—Hemingway resorts to the fakery of having Santiago identify him at once as a male. In an effort, perhaps, to make this bit of fakery more believable, Hemingway has Santiago recall an experience with marlin in which he was able to distinguish the male from the female.

> He remembered the time he had hooked one of a pair of marlin. The male fish always let the female fish feed first and the hooked fish, the female, made a wild, panic-stricken, despairing fight that soon exhausted her, and all the time the male had stayed with her, crossing the line and circling with her on the surface. He had stayed so close that the old man was afraid he would cut the line with his tail which was sharp as a scythe. . . . When the old man had gaffed her and clubbed her, . . . and then, . . . hoisted her aboard, the male fish had

stayed by the side of the boat. Then while the old man was clearing the lines and preparing the harpoon, the male fish jumped high into the air beside the boat to see where the female was and then went down deep . . . He was beautiful, the old man remembered, and he had stayed.

Santiago's story of the devoted male marlin actually creates more problems than it solves. It is a preposterous piece of natural history, combining sentimentality and inexact observation. The Associate Curator of Fishes of the American Museum of Natural History, who was also a friend of Hemingway's, Francesca LaMonte, noticed an interesting parallel between Santiago's story and one Hemingway recounts in his marlin essay in *American Big Game Fishing:*

> Another time . . . my wife caught a 74-pound white marlin which was followed by three other marlin all through the fight. These three refused bait but stayed with the female fish until she was gaffed and brought aboard. Then they went down.

Miss LaMonte comments on this story that "You will note that the sex of the other fishes is not stated." Hemingway has Santiago incredibly enough identify the uncaught fish as males but in his essay he is more realistic.

Santiago and his fish are yoked by Hemingway's method of using the animal to epitomize some aspect of the man. The result, as Carlos Baker admiringly puts it, is "gallantry against gallantry." It is in fact more nearly fakery against fakery: a make-believe super-fish duelling a make-believe super-fisherman.

It must be conceded that leaving aside these two formidable adversaries, there are brilliant flashes of Hemingway realism in *The Old Man and the Sea.* The sharks, for example, are depicted with remarkable vividness as they rush the dead marlin and savagely tear it apart. The shovel-nosed sharks with their "wide, flattened, shovel-pointed heads . . . and their slitted yellow cat-like eyes" are made "good and true enough" so that they are convincing as sharks *and* as embodiments of pure evil.

With the mako shark, however, Hemingway has not wholly resisted the impulse to fake. He has claimed for the mako that he can swim "as fast as the fastest fish in the sea" and equipped him with eight rows of teeth "shaped like a man's fingers when they are crisped like claws. They were nearly as long as . . . fingers . . . and they had razor-sharp cutting edges on both sides." E. M. Schroeder, of the Harvard Museum of Comparative Zoology, an authority on the sharks of the Atlantic, and other shark experts seriously doubt that the mako is as fast as the fastest fish. And they find support from Hemingway who in an article in *Game Fish of the World* says that the mako can "run faster than most," and in another article mentions the tuna and wahoo as "the fastest fish in the sea."

To describe the mako as having eight rows of teeth, as Hemingway does, is a great deal like saying that a five-year-old child has forty or so teeth. Only two rows of the shark's teeth are functional; the others are replacements which become functional as the forward teeth are lost or destroyed. Also, according to Professor Voss, only the main teeth in the mid part of the shark's jaw are as long, slender, and sharp as Hemingway describes *all* the teeth as being. Just as Santiago and his fish are given extraordinary powers they could not in fact possess, the biggest and most dangerous of the sharks, the mako, is made more menacing than he actually is.

II

Why are these inaccuracies of any consequence? No one thinks less of Keats's sonnet "On First Looking into Chapman's Homer" because in it Keats confused "stout Cortez" with Balboa as the discoverer of the Pacific; nor have the numerous anachronisms in Shakespeare's plays diminished his reputation or our enjoyment of his plays. Don't we read imaginative literature with an entirely different attitude toward fact from the one with which we consult an encyclopedia? The answer must be yes, but a qualified yes. We do not read either Keats or Shakespeare with the same expectations or assumptions as those we have when we read Hemingway. Hemingway is above all a realist; his aim had always been to communicate the facts exactly; and his reputation rests squarely on his success in doing so. As we read a Hemingway story or novel, his preoccupation with factual detail is immediately apparent. It is nowhere more apparent than in his heroes' respect for accuracy and a firm grip on the facts. Frederic Henry speaks for Hemingway, too, in what is probably the best known passage in *A Farewell to Arms* when he says: "Abstract words such as glory, honor, courage, or hallow were obscene beside the concrete names of villages, the number of roads, the names of rivers, the numbers of regiments and the dates." In short, the facts. And, likewise, those characters whom Hemingway places in contrast to his heroes are most readily distinguished not by their lack of honor, their insensitivity, or their political allegiances but by their sloppy handling of the facts. There is no clearer example of this than the tourist couple at the end of *The Old Man and the Sea* who look down into the water from the Terrace, see the skeleton of Santiago's great marlin, and ignorantly mistake it for a shark.

And Hemingway saw himself as a realist, too. His task in *The Old*

Man and the Sea, as he saw it, was to give us a *real* old man, a *real* fish, and a *real* sea that would, if he had made them truly and well, mean many things. This is a reasonable definition of the goal of any realistic writer and provides us with a useful gauge of Hemingway's achievement. However, many critics have turned Hemingway's gauge upside down and upon discovering that the story of the old Cuban fisherman's ordeal can mean many things have praised it without troubling themselves to discover if the old man, the fish, and the sea are indeed "real," if they are indeed made "good and true." [1]

The realism of Hemingway's first published stories is not an arbitrarily selected technique: it is an inevitable part of his world view. Confronted by the violence and meaninglessness of the world he saw as a boy in upper Michigan, as an 18-year-old police reporter on the *Kansas City Star,* and as a young man on the Italian front in World War I, in the Greco-Turkish War, and in the cities of Europe in the 1920's, he cultivated a bare, stoical, tight-lipped style that was an ideal instrument for exploring that God-abandoned world. The bullfighters, expatriates, soldiers, boxers, and guerillas were rendered vividly but truly and objectively. And their stance, if they were among the initiated, was much like the style that depicted them, one of tense control, like Nick Adams' trout holding itself steady against the current of the Big Two-Hearted River.

But the style has gone soft in *The Old Man and the Sea* because the view of the world has gone soft. Santiago's universe is not the chaotic universe in which Nick Adams, Frederic Henry, Jake Barnes, and Robert Jordan encountered meaningless violence and evil. It is more nearly a cozy universe in which fish have nobility and loyalty and other virtues no one since St. Francis of Assisi—and least of all Ernest Hemingway—would have suspected them of. It is a universe so chummy that the hero calls various birds his brothers. The sharks introduce a semblance of evil into this warm universe, but it tends to be a stagey, melodramatic evil almost too villainous to be believable. The same is true of the big Portuguese man-of-war trailing its poisonous tentacles as it sails by Santiago's skiff fully six months before an animal this size would normally appear in Cuban waters.

The soft, fuzzy tone of *The Old Man and the Sea* reaches its nadir in that scene shortly after sunset when the incredible old man, still being towed by his incredible fish, looks into the heavens and sees the

---

[1] Much has been written about Hemingway's technique as a realist: his extraordinary skill in communicating the feel of experience. But with one exception, no one has extensively tested the reality of his fiction in terms of its correspondence to verifiable fact. The exception is Arturo Barea's "Not Spain but Hemingway," *Horizon* [England], III (May 1941), 350–61. [Reprinted: Carlos Baker, *Hemingway and His Critics,* New York, 1961.]

first star of this universe shining out. Hemingway comments: "He did not know the name of Rigel but he saw it and knew soon they would all be out and he would have all his distant friends." This cosmic camaraderie is patently false and forced. This is not the violent, chaotic world that young Hemingway discovered and explored with a style whittled from a walnut stick. In that world the stars were cold and remote—as stars really are. In the world of *The Old Man and the Sea,* they are "friends" whom the author in a patronizing intrusion identifies for us—incorrectly. Rigel does not appear in Cuban skies at sunset in September but some five hours after Santiago sees it. It is, perhaps, a trifling error, which, even if we happen to be aware of it, does not surprise us in a novel in which so much else is inexactly observed or tricked out in an effort to extort more feeling than a reasonable person would find there.

The honest, disciplined quest for "the way it was" finally ran down. *The Old Man and the Sea* stands as an end point of that quest. Yet it is not without greatness. To call it an inferior Hemingway novel still leaves it standing well above most other novels of our time. But some of its greatness is that of a monument serving to remind us of earlier glories.

New World, Old Myths

by Claire Rosenfield

Criticism has accustomed us to recognize the "American myth" in William Faulkner's "The Bear" and in Ernest Hemingway's *The Old Man and the Sea*. Whether that myth exploited the confrontation between man—the innocent, the child-like, the "American Adam"—and "wild nature" [1]—the huge animal, the monstrous fish—or simply emphasized the "distinctly American" flavor of exaggeration in "tall tales" that paraded animals of extraordinary size or endurance, we eagerly nationalized it first and only then did we analyze it. But any study of the folk tale—products not only of peasant or rustic (or prairie) societies but also of primitive or tribal societies[2]—would reveal the same motif, the same confrontation between the hero and a large indigenous animal he both fears and admires. Perhaps more interesting is why the American writer persistently chooses this almost universal motif, this subject that some would consider a regression to folk materials, this pattern that has led Leslie Fiedler rightly to point out that the American hero is in fact or in spirit a child.[3] Nor is it a question of American civilization developing "by means of a return to wild nature," [4] for it had never really been there in its expressive works. Its culture began *in medias res* with a literature

[1] Frederick I. Carpenter, " 'The American Myth': Paradise (To Be) Regained," *PMLA*, LXXIV (1959), 605.

[2] By "peasant society" I mean a small, isolated, homogeneous group, each member of which may be as illiterate as any tribesman but whose community, as Robert Redfield points out, "is only a part-community, his society is incomplete without the town or city, and he himself sees his world so as to include urban things and people. . . . a peasant village carries on its own internal life in part by institutions and through long-established expectations arising from the town or city." Both peasant societies and tribal ones, however, are "Folk societies." See Robert Redfield, "Tribe, Peasant, and City," *Human Nature and the Study of Society: The Papers of Robert Redfield*, ed. by Margaret Park Redfield (Chicago and London, 1962), I, 287.

[3] Leslie A. Fiedler, *Love and Death in the American Novel* (New York, 1960).

[4] Carpenter, *op. cit.*

essentially European, often deeply sophisticated and urbane in tone, subject, and style. Once the literature of the New World freed itself from its Puritan emphasis upon sermons, spiritual autobiography, and moral tracts, once its novels divorced themselves from the sentimental tradition that hounded books like *Charlotte Temple* and from the Gothic tradition that pervaded Charles Brockden Brown's *Ormond* —and, indeed, all those lesser works in which the terror *was* of Germany and *not* of the soul—then our literature began as near the beginning, as near oral conventions, as a literate culture is now allowed to go. It exploited folk materials which it often placed in a local— hence prairie—setting. Some of its greatest and most representative novels absorbed a very conventional content that only seemed American because the European literary experience in which the early colonists continued to immerse themselves had been so long estranged from its roots, from its awareness of folk patterns.[5] And because these patterns seemed so genuinely American (when, in actuality, they are primarily human), they persisted both in extremely intricate form like "The Bear" and in highly stylized prose like *The Old Man and the Sea*. What is American, then, is the persistence of the folk motif, not the motif itself. Moreover, that it endured for the wrong reason— because of its emotional value rather than its human validity—is also distinctly American.

If completely at odds in style and structure, the two short novels under discussion are more than superficially alike in content. Both are stories which deal with situations of crisis in the lives of the protagonists, crises which are marked by rites of passage, threshold events that bridge the gulf from one state of physical, social, and intellectual being into another. In both, a much older man—simple, intuitive, wise in the life of Nature—acts as a mentor for an innocent "apprentice" upon whose ability to learn and whose devotion to craft his own personal immortality in part depends. Each novel explores a totemic relationship, an association between a man and an object in nature. And in each the totemic relationship provides a stage upon which religious and/or social meanings dramatize themselves. At once game and rite, each hunt exerts a symbolic meaning beyond the physical destruction of a remarkable wild creature.

The Old Man and the Sea begins eighty-four days after the old fisherman's last catch. The boy Manolin, the apprentice whom he has long regarded "with confident loving eyes," who had shared the first

---

[5] European "frontiers" had long ceased to exist, forcing its people to substitute complex social monsters for simple real ones or go hunting in new worlds. So Chancery Court in *Bleak House* may be described as a devouring animal, but the symbolic dimension and the *genre* have completely annihilated our awareness of oral convention.

forty barren days, has been forced by his parents to "another boat which caught three good fish the first week." [6] In their mutual reminiscences concerning the past the reader discovers that Manolin first accompanied the old man Santiago when the former was five years old, that the boy is lovingly described as "already a man" in his knowledge of things of the sea, that the pupil claims to remember everything "from when . . . [they] first went together." During the intensity of the old man's ordeal, when for three days he tries to land the largest marlin ever seen in that area, he longs again and again for the boy's presence, as much for companionship as for assistance. Now he has only himself and the sea to talk to. Every new crisis recalls Manolin's worth. When his hand is cramped by the coil of rope, he wishes the boy were there to rub it or, later, to wet the abrasive hemp. As he approaches port with the "half-fish," the catch partially consumed by sharks, he meditates upon the others' response to his absence. "There is only the boy to worry, of course. But I am sure he would have confidence" (115).

The imagery of spiritual kinship makes it possible for the reader to see causal relationship in apparently illogical juxtapositions. " 'I wish the boy were here and that I had some salts' " (56) not only marks his need and love for the boy and the necessity for making palatable the raw tuna he must eat to preserve his strength but also indicates the connection between the eater and the eaten, the fisherman who must fish to eat and eat to fish, the nourisher of the body and that of the spirit. He wishes that he could "feed the fish" he has hooked because he is his brother. Denied his teacher because his hostile parents regard that teacher as "unlucky," the boy asserts his bond by bringing food for the old man to eat and some sardines for the catch. At first the food he provides substitutes for that which the old man cannot provide for himself; in the end, it marks the boy's assumption of the responsibility for nourishing the man who had long fostered his spirit. Fishing, exactly that process by which the man has established communion with the boy, who does bring him food, is part of the cycle that unites all things in nature; it both feeds and destroys. "Fishing kills me exactly as it keeps me alive" (106).

No critic would debate the spiritual kinship between man and boy; the latter inherits not the blood but the knowledge of the former. Nor would anyone longer deny that the fish is a totem animal. As A. R. Radcliffe-Brown posited in 1929, the totem animal of a group is often the one upon which one's subsistence depends. [7] Both man and boy

---

[6] Ernest Hemingway, *The Old Man and the Sea*, The Scribner Library (New York, 1952), p. 9. All subsequent quotations of ten words or more will provide pagination within the text.

[7] A. R. Radcliffe-Brown, "The Sociological Theory of Totemism," *Structure and Function in Primitive Society* (London, 1952), pp. 117–32. As Radcliffe-Brown

regard their numerous prey as part of the same order of created beings, part of the same human society. Having once hooked the female of a pair of marlins, they pity the reaction of the distraught male. "That was the saddest thing I ever saw with them. . . . The boy was sad too and we begged her pardon and butchered her promptly" (50). To the fish he has just hooked after eighty-four "unlucky" days Santiago says " 'I love you and respect you very much. But I will kill you dead before this day ends' " (54). He calls the fish both "friend" and "brother" and regrets that he must "live on the sea and kill [his] true brothers." How demeaning that those who will feed upon him will not be worthy of him. "There is no one worthy of eating him from the manner of his behaviour and his great dignity" (75). Not simply a "great fish," his captor assigns to the marlin the quality of human thought: he is "following his own plan" as he circles; the old man must "convince" his prey; the marlin may "decide to stay another night." The very desire to prove worthy of this creature's admiration provides additional strength to Santiago's weakening body. "Let him think I am more man than I am and I will be so" (64). The same fish once dead and lashed to his boat is no less dignified, no less a part of communal life. "With his mouth shut and his tail straight up and down we sail like brothers" (99). When the gallant opponent is first mutilated by the sharks, Santiago thinks "it was as though he himself were hit." And when these "bad smelling" sharks, these "scavengers as well as killers," devour the marlin, Santiago can only murmur " 'I'm sorry, fish.' " If the totem animal of a group also reflects the society in some way, then this noble marlin reflects the qualities Santiago possesses, admires, and wishes to hand on to the boy: nobility, "greatness," and "glory," endurance, dignity, beauty.

And in his defeat, in his desecration by scavengers, he symbolizes Santiago, who is ridiculed by younger fishermen, who is regarded as "strange" and "unlucky," whose final triumph is destroyed by sharks, and who, broken in body and spirit, a skeleton of his former self, can only sleep and dream of the lions of his youth.

The development of his story through time has little to do with the greater complexity of William Faulkner's emphasis upon initiation and totemism. What determines the complexity is not that we see the relationship between Ike and Sam Fathers progress for seven fall and six spring hunts and that of Manolin and Santiago for two short spaces of less than twelve hours each, but rather that Faulkner consciously exploits what Hemingway only peripherally understands. Ike senses that he is entering in a new life when his day to enter the woods comes;

---

himself later indicates, this is not the only reason why a particular choice is made.

it "seemed to him that he was witnessing his own birth." [8] In order to hunt Old Ben, the bear, he must serve "his apprenticeship in the woods which would prove him worthy to be a hunter . . ." (200). He enters "his novitiate to the true wilderness with Sam beside him as he had begun his apprenticeship in miniature to manhood after the rabbits and such with Sam beside him" (201). Half Indian chief, half Negro slave, Sam Fathers knows intuitively how each step in Ike's initiation must take shape and conveys that knowledge often without words. From Sam he learns that, although Old Ben has been to camp to see him, he cannot see the bear until he has relinquished his gun in order that "all ancient rules and balances of hunter and hunted had been abrogated" (211). By submitting completely to the wilderness, the pathless, ageless wall of trees, by leaving behind the mechanical aids of civilization, his watch and compass, by proceeding "as Sam had coached and drilled him"—only then does he see the bear and partake of its secret life. Moreover, Sam's mysterious affinity to Nature anticipates each step before its explanation in action: he knows why the boy doesn't shoot the bear when he confronts it squarely; he knows the dead colt was not killed by Old Ben but by the dog that will eventually corner the bear; he senses that his own life and Old Ben's are tied in a mystic unity and will snap together. With no true familial ties, *"no children, no people, none of his blood anywhere above earth that he would ever meet again"* (218), he bequeathes his knowledge to the boy. Ike, who hardly knew his own father, first manifests his loyalty by disobeying his guardian and cousin, "his kinsman, his father almost," McCaslin Edmonds, in order to stay with the dying Sam. Later he protects Boon when his cousin Cass fails to understand the necessary continuity in Sam's death. Finally, he gives up his birthright to assume Sam's role in the diminishing woods. Spiritual kinship has superseded real ties, has filled the vacuum left both by death and by ancestral depravity.

Old Ben is the symbol both of the bigness of the woods and of its destruction. And, as such, he acquires a more than human status.

> It loomed and towered in his dreams before he ever saw the unaxed woods where it left its crooked print, shaggy, tremendous, red-eyed, not malevolent but just big . . . ; too big for the very country which was its constricting scope. It was as if the boy had already divined what his senses and intellect had not encompassed yet: that doomed wilderness whose edges were being constantly and punily gnawed at by men with plows and axes . . . , men myriad and nameless even to one another in the land where the old bear had earned a name,

[8] William Faulkner, "The Bear," *The Portable Faulkner*, ed. with an introduction by Malcolm Cowley, rev. ed. (New York, 1967), p. 201. All quotations of ten or more words will be cited in the text.

and through which ran not even a mortal beast but an anachronism
indomitable and invincible out of an old death time, a phantom,
epitome and apotheosis of the old wild life which the little puny
humans swarmed and hacked at in a fury of abhorrence and fear,
like pygmies about the ankles of a drowsing elephant . . . (199).

His very name is a mark of hunter's respect; he has "earned" it, "a
definite designation like a living man." Like Santiago's reverence for the
fish, Sam attributes to Old Ben human curiosity and ability: the desire to survey the camp to see " 'who's here, who's new in camp this
year.' " He's " 'the head bear. . . . the man.' " All congregate "as if
they were meeting an appointment with another human being" (214).
Even Major de Spain, the Southern gentleman and hunter who believes erroneously that Old Ben has killed his colt, recognizes the bear's
superior powers. " 'I'm disappointed in him. He has broken the
rules. . . . I didn't think he would have done that. He has killed
mine and McCaslin's dogs, but that was all right. We gambled the dogs
against him; we gave each other warning. But now he has come into
my house and destroyed my property, out of season too. He broke the
rules' " (217). To him, Old Ben has purposely ignored the temporal
and spatial limitations placed upon him by the rules of the game-hunt.

In the juxtaposition of Old Ben's sacrifice, Lion's mutilation, and
Sam's collapse and death we must recognize an artistic chain defining
totemic causality. Sam "lay there—the copper-brown, almost hairless
body, the old man's body, the old man, the wild man not even one
generation from the woods, childless, kinless, peopleless—motionless,
his eyes open but no longer looking at any of them" (245). Old Ben
in death lay "with his eyes open too." Like Sam, denied his chief's role
because his land has been sold and his blood diluted with the blood
of slaves, Old Ben belonged to the past aristocrats of the diminishing
wilderness. Like Sam, he was old and alone: "widowered, childless, and
absolved of mortality—old Priam reft of his old wife and outlived all
his sons." Both participate in a mutual life, contingent upon a past
grandeur within the timeless woods. Neither can survive the degrada-
tion imposed by a different culture.

Thus the totemic animal in "The Bear" is chosen less because he
is "eatable" than because, as writers on totemism point out, his
situation and his world have an intimate connection with the function-
ing society. The very existence of two hunts proclaims a hierarchy of
birth joined to that of skill. During the fall hunt, the game is deer
or bear; the participants, the proven hunters of Southern white landed
families. In the spring, they celebrate at one session the widely dis-
parate birthdays of Major de Spain and General Compson. ". . . Boon
and the Negroes (and the boy too now) fished and shot squirrels and

ran the coons and cats, because the proven hunters, not only Major de Spain and old General Compson . . . but even McCaslin and Walter Ewell who were still young enough, scorned such, other than shooting the wild gobblers with pistols for wagers or to test their marksmanship" (209). As "the man" among animals Old Ben deserves their special attention; the last day of the autumn period is devoted to him. Because of his stature only the "best" are allowed to participate. But the best are those whose superiority is based in a social structure that flourished on slavery, whose wealth is derived from the ownership of land "bought" or stolen from the Indians and from the cultivation of that same land by human chattel. So in its pattern of participation the fall hunt mirrors the hierarchial society. It is also a ritual reenactment of the rape of the land, which the vanishing wilderness recalls.

We see, however, that Ike's ancestors who determined his hereditary role in holding the land, could not provide him with models for emulation or respect. His own grandfather had fathered a child by a slave girl who was both his property and his daughter. In repudiating his land, which he claims should be held by all men in common, Ike in effect separates himself from his personal history. That grandfather's immorality is but the final act of deterioration which telescopes several sins: the mythic disobedience of Adam, the historical crime of slavery, the national crime of private property. For Ike to make Sam Fathers the progenitor of a spiritual patrimony is to deny the real one. Those "proven hunters," who caused Sam, the chief's son to be "peopleless" and "landless," whose sport pursues Old Ben—"Priam reft of his old wife and outlived all his sons"—these men themselves leave no sons to inherit the fruits of their crimes.

The failure of Ike's marriage, his future celibacy, is predictable not simply because he rejects his fathers, not simply because he adopts a deeper tie, but also because his intimate connection with nature demands it. Like his mentor he must be "childless, kinless, peopleless"; like the totem animal, whose woods are annihilated by a mechanical civilization, he must be "landless"; like both he must reflect, not Christian, but primitive values. The image of the crawling serpent is used once to describe the small train inaugurated by the lumber company that eventually denudes the land; as such, its corruption is implied. On his last trip to camp before the timber is cut, Ike sees a hissing snake, a creature that his culture invests with all the connotations of evil because of its role in seducing Eve. At first he recognizes it as "ancient and accursed about the earth, fatal and solitary," its smell "evocative of all knowledge and an old weariness and of pariah-hood and of death." But then he imagines it in its supposed prelapsarian shape, an erect creature moving as if human and on two legs.

The elevation of the head did not change as it began to glide away
from him, moving erect yet off the perpendicular as if the head and
that elevated third were complete and all: an entity walking on two
feet and free of all laws of mass and balance, and should have been
because even now he could not quite believe that all that shift and
flow of shadow behind that walking head could have been one snake:
going and then gone . . . . (318)

That is, he gradually sees it not as a symbol of Adam's fall, crawling
on its belly, but as tradition assigned it before its great offense. He has
removed the negative value that his culture insists upon. In hailing it
with raised hand, he follows the earlier form and the strange language
he learned from Sam Fathers: " 'Chief' he said: 'Grandfather.' " This
greeting is not the ironic recognition of Ike that his own religious
and social tradition is damned. Rather, his change in vision indicates
that he now accepts Sam at once as a teacher and guide in matters of
the hunt and as an ancestor in a primitive religious tradition, a tradition older and more meaningful than the salvation-oriented one into
which he was born. He soon clings to this tradition because, in uniting
all men and animals as brothers, it is without taint of hierarchy, ownership, and innate depravity.

Especially in Faulkner's ability to pursue all the ramifications of
totemism to the larger social and religious community we can mark
his superiority to Hemingway. Both present primitive religions, a
single and harmonious cosmos in which the self seeks no independent
identity apart from its environment. So when Santiago's left hand is
cut and cramps, he addresses it dispassionately as if it had no special
link to his body, were no part of a human whole that is separate and
unique within a physical environment. In fact, whereas the fish is a
"brother," worthy of respect, his left hand is a "traitor," "something
worthless." Nor do I mean to imply anything pejorative when I emphasize the "primitive." Rather, these characters possess a world view
very like that attributed to an early stage in the evolutionary cycle,
a stage that can and does remain a part of the most highly developed
religion. If, as Robert Bellah theorizes, "primitive *religious* action is
characterized not . . . by worship, nor, as we shall see, by sacrifice, but
by identification, 'participation,' acting-out," [9] then Hemingway's old
man is intently engaged in such action. To address the fish as "friend"
and "brother," to identify himself with it indicates that for him, as
for the primitive, the "distance between man and mythical being disappears altogether in the moment of ritual." [10] The catch has all the

[9] Robert Bellah, "Religious Evolution," *American Sociological Review*, XXIX,
3 (June, 1964), 363. I have relied heavily upon this excellent formulation for
the distinctions I make among stages of religion.
[10] *Ibid.*

external manifestations of ritual: action follows certain forms; it is isolated from the ordinary world temporally and spatially; it is calculated to provide its participant with some strange power (i.e., the power of the marlin). In its final stage the catch takes the form of a circle which gradually diminishes in size and in depth. "But the circles were much shorter now and from the way the line slanted he could tell the fish had risen steadily while he swam" (87). Though he often reiterates his own suffering, he does not neglect to remind us as readers of the same suffering endured by the fish. The "no-time" of ritual is approximated when the intensity of that suffering causes him to become light-headed, to lose the sense of continuity and reality; his experience seems to be a dream. Having lost his fish to the sharks, he endures whatever limitations his exhaustion, his age, his aloneness, his few weapons —all the conditions, in fact, of his existence—impose. He becomes transformed insofar as he is now able to accept his failure; like the initiates involved in a ritual, he has come to terms symbolically with ". . . the 'immemorial misdirection of human life.'" [11]

Unfortunately Ernest Hemingway does not perceive the variety that life forces upon man's expression of religious behavior nor the abundant permutations even the simplest faith may take. For him the dogma of Christianity and its enactment in ritual define the word; and its verbal forms are charged with an emotion largely inflated, meaningless, bombastic. So the author, whose American expatriates usually recognize the validity of tradition within the societies through which they aimlessly ramble, pays some lip service to the old man's nominal Christianity. Though Santiago is "not religious," he promises to make a pilgrimage to the Virgin of Cobre should he catch the marlin, a pilgrimage to that Virgin whose picture in his hut is a reminder of his long-dead wife rather than the image of a transcendent power. He prays not for his own salvation, as a Christian would, but for "the death of this fish. Wonderful though he is."

It is when the author's indiscriminate love of masculine games merges with his distrust of abstraction—whether religious, sexual, or patriotic—that he renders trivial the power of the situation he has created. The reader need not fathom the relationship between games and the development of religions from the bottomless past to admit that games and rites have precise similarities: a regularized pattern of behavior, an actual or psychological withdrawal from the everyday world of time and space, a temporary release from anxiety, an emphasis upon communal activity. Though in our society the one partakes of the serious situations of life and the other, of the profane, in

[11] *Ibid.*

each, man is "carried outside himself and diverted from his ordinary occupation and preoccupation." [12]

The image of the game dominates beginning, middle, and end, the most minor as well as the most potentially moving moments of the narrative. The novel's opening underscores Santiago's multiple influence upon the boy, his guidance in the intricacies both of the sometime sport by which the old man earns his bread and of the foreign amusement called "the baseball." [13] When no danger threatens within the action, a gentle humor emanates from his ability to pontificate upon "the baseball," to recall the magical presence in Cuba of its greatest "heroes," to derive satisfaction from the rumor that the father of "the great DiMaggio was a fisherman." And the boy's admiration for Santiago's uniqueness within his natural vocation and for Durocher and Mike Gonzalez as managers of the sport tend to fuse and confuse a way of life with a mode of entertainment. Whereas "faith" is necessary for catching fish, especially when one is supposed to be "unlucky," "faith" is also a concomitant to the skill of the Yankees; one must have faith in their ability to win and *they will win*. To remember the ancient tie in archaic religions between games of chance and divination[14] is to understand this old man's prelogical desire that his disciple "buy a terminal of the lottery with an eighty-five" (17). The day that he goes to pursue his "big fish" is his eighty-fifth without luck. He at once assigns a predictive value to the lottery and makes the game a symbolic reflection of his own human situation. The excruciating simplicity that functions to lessen his success as a consciousness through which we experience the events of the narrative is, paradoxically, made credible by his childlike concern for "the great DiMaggio," by his exaggerated respect for "gambling," by his mystical belief in luck. If Manolin, who has gone to a "lucky" boat, were his son, he would "gamble," take the boy out on the eighty-fifth day with a confidence equal to that with which he places money upon the number of a lottery.

Once the life-and-death struggle between man and fish begins, once the old man becomes obsessed by the intimacy between himself, who was "born to be a fisherman," and the victim, then the story demands some recognition of the mystery involved in each human destiny. But

[12] Emile Durkheim, *The Elementary Forms of the Religious Life,* trans. by Joseph Ward Swain (Glencoe, Illinois, n.d.), p. 383.

[13] Hemingway's attempt to approximate the tone of the Spanish language in his English dialogue betrays him into an unpleasant artificiality beyond the demands of artifice—as is equally true in *For Whom The Bell Tolls.*

[14] "It is commonly thought by many peoples that the winners of games of chance have received supernatural or magical aid." See John M. Roberts *et al.,* "Games in Culture," *American Anthropologist,* LXI, 4 (August, 1959), 601.

Hemingway's nagging suspicions about RELIGION seduce him into a constant apology that takes the form of overt statement or metaphorical reduction. First, the old man must insist that he is "not religious"; he must manifest this fact by saying his prayers "mechanically" or "automatically"; he must, in effect, justify his lapse into belief. For his author forgets that he is not Jake Barnes; he does not have to rationalize from a sophisticated perspective of the world his apparently illogical combination of Christian prayer and pagan participation in rites of the kill. And having dramatized a genuinely religious man—albeit a devotee of a primitive religion—Hemingway's initial instinct to connect church and society, the religious and the social, within the boat is sound. But his emphatically male bias makes the purposive mingling of game and rite ridiculous; not only has the game he chooses no suggestion of cult participation or identification (as the bullfight has in *The Sun Also Rises*) but also the reader finds it impossible to spiritualize the too-human celebrities that he has read about in sports pages and gossip columns. Human interdependence is reduced to a diversion. Perhaps it is artistically valid that the old man, who earlier was the prophet of "the baseball," should lament on his second day tied to the dying fish because he does "not know the result of the *juegos.* . . ." That he values his endurance, however, because it makes him "worthy of the great DiMaggio who does all things perfectly even with the pain of the bone spur in his heel" (68), that he dilutes life and death—even that of fighting cocks—to such thinness, indicates that Hemingway has failed to gage the possibility of the comparison. Masculine admiration substitutes for aesthetic judgment. When the sharks come, Santiago's brooding upon the death of the marlin seems perverse. "But I must think . . . because it is all I have left. That and baseball" (103). Given the quality of his previous thought, such a juxtaposition is gratuitous. When "sin" becomes the concept to occupy his thoughts, he rejects it because "there are people who are paid to do it . . . [He was] born to be a fisherman as the fish was born to be a fish. San Pedro was a fisherman as was the father of the great DiMaggio" (105). Santiago knows that a man who was "born to be a fisherman" is not adept in meditating upon sin, but Hemingway cannot resist the temptation to "yoke by violence together" the persons of Saint Peter and the "father of the great DiMaggio." The reader senses that the apotheosis of the fisherman is not far distant. The image calculated to turn the elderly protagonist into a Christ-figure does come, but the author intrudes awkwardly into the text, probably to soften the patent attempt at manipulating our responses. " '*Ay,*' he said aloud. There is no translation for this word and perhaps it is just a noise such as a man might make, involuntarily, feeling the nail go through his hands and into the wood" (107). The disturbing violation of tone stems both from the unnecessary allusion to a sympathetic culture hero and from the movement from Santiago's consciousness to Hemingway's. The consequent sentimentalization of the old man is harder to accept than his fabulous endurance. Again, the Christimage ludicrously jars our awareness, primarily because the old fisherman has already canonized the great DiMaggio. Nor does his insistence that he thinks about baseball in order to take his mind off his suffering reconcile us to the banal range of his perceptions. The context in which rites and rules function together to characterize the ordered world of Spain and to serve as a contrast to the disorder of the Jake Barnes circle does not exist here. Since the old man is very much in harmony with his physical environment, his religious world view is debased to the level of the game that, unfortunately, is only a game.

Avoiding the temptation to dramatize the hunt from the too simple eyes of Sam Fathers, whose knowledge, like Santiago's, is limited to his intuitions, William Faulkner chooses as the center of narrative consciousness the boy Ike. Even as a ten-year-old child he is acutely aware of historical and social phenomena. The hunting of bear is no longer required for the subsistence of any group. Though it has become a sport, the reader is never allowed to forget its religious implications. Described as a "yearly pageant-rite of the old bear's furious immortality" (200), it has no part of the routine of our time-space world; clocks and compasses are useless in the "great gloom of ancient woods." Instead, the game is set against the bigger life of Nature; it occurs at the "year's death." Moreover, Faulkner makes a subtle distinction among his characters; there are those for whom sharing in the hunt no longer confers any spiritual value and those for whom the ritual anticipates some personal crisis. The swampers, the townsmen in new clothes who gather to watch the kill do not count at all; they are mere spectators of the "yearly rendezvous." Ike's belief in its unique mystery invests the very drinking of liquor with a meaning relevant to this "ancient and immitigable contest according to ancient and immitigable rules":

> There was always a bottle present, so that it would seem to him that those fine fierce instants of heart and brain and courage and wiliness and speed were concentrated and distilled into that brown liquor which not women, not boys and children, but only hunters drank, drinking it moderately, humbly even, not with the pagan's base and baseless hope of acquiring thereby the virtues of cunning and strength and speed but in salute to them. Thus it seemed to him on this December morning not only natural but actually fitting that this should have begun with whiskey. (198)

The use of phrases like "it would seem to him" indicates that it is Ike's eye that suffuses the event with solemnity. "To him, they were going not to hunt bear and deer but to keep yearly rendezvous with the bear which they did not even intend to kill" (199). Given these assumptions, how he and Sam Fathers act out the various stages of initiation becomes one subject of the first three parts of the narrative. He must discover that this world in which all the ancient rules and balances of hunter and hunted had been abrogated" (211) provides him with the possibility of coming to terms symbolically or really with his personal and historical past. Sam's marking him with the blood of his first buck is one link in the long chain of rites that will ultimately connect him to the past of Nature and divorce him from that of Western history.

The other Southerners, who regard the hunt as an exercise of skill and sportsmanship rather than an acting out of mythical events, possess inferior knowledge for interpreting facts. Rules not rites dominate their world. When Major de Spain learns about the separation of the frantic mare from her colt, he immediately assumes that Old Ben has broken "the rules." The body of the colt causes the proven hunters to continue to deceive themselves, but the boy does not realize until much later why Sam understands and they do not. "Afterward the boy realized that they also should have known then what killed the colt as well as Sam Fathers did. But that was neither the first nor the last time he had seen men rationalize from and even act upon their mis-conceptions" (218). Finally, Cass and Major de Spain misjudge the role that Sam's willed death plays in the rite. In a harmonious cosmos where "the distance between man and mythical being, which was at best slight, disappears altogether in the moment of ritual," [15] Boon's killing Old Ben during the "yearly pageant-rite" is the symbolic killing of Sam. Whether Boon does in fictional actuality kill Sam, as Cass believes and as Faulkner later stated,[16] is ultimately irrelevant for the wilderness world. That Cass insists upon knowing, even while he claims that he would have done the same had Sam requested it, is his carrying into the woods, into the space of identification and participa-tion, the ethical standards of a society that emphasizes a "responsible" self. He cannot accept Sam's death as the boy does, as the logical con-sequence of ritual action, but rather regards it as a crime against a social structure that mediates between orthodox Christianity and some divinely sanctioned moral order presumed to be objective.

Until he is sixteen, then, the boy immerses his Christian self in ritual action. Twice a year for two-week periods he moves from the daily routine of his culture, from a society whose religious values are ex-

[15] Bellah, *op. cit.*, p. 363.
[16] Frederick L. Gwynn and Joseph L. Blotner, eds., *Faulkner in the University: Class Conferences at the University of Virginia 1957–1958* (Charlottesville, 1959), pp. 10 and 47.

pressed in worldly institutions, from a belief in a transcendent deity and in individual salvation by grace and in man's corrupted nature,[17] into the timeless woods. And he goes influenced by his own class's idea of the hunt as a game. Faulkner, however, insists again and again upon the boy's unlearned response, his anticipation that has nothing to do with either godlike foreknowledge or Calvinist predestination (though Part IV may make the critic think so) or with the rules of the game. His intuition is similar to what W. E. H. Stanner has called The Dreaming: the tendency among primitive religious men to prefigure in "a time out of time" extraordinary creatures, both human and animal, who "have capacities beyond those of ordinary men as well as being the progenitors and creators of many particular things in the world." [18] So Old Ben is perceived imaginatively long before his physical presence is seen.

> It ran in his knowledge before he ever saw it. It loomed and towered in his dreams before he ever saw the unaxed woods where it left its crooked print, shaggy, tremendous, red-eyed, not malevolent but just big. . . . (199)

> It seemed to him that he could see them, the two of them, shadowy in the limbo from which time emerged and became time: the old bear absolved of mortality and himself who shared a little of it. (208)

Like the no-time of "The Dreaming," the mental experience explains what happens in the real fictional world; Old Ben, as mythical ancestor, and his final destruction by puny men have already happened before they are acted out in ritual.

Ultimately what his heritage denotes as a game becomes for him a way of being; momentary ritual transforms life. Nor is it mere chance that the last hunt must be extended beyond the usual temporal limits of two weeks. Such an extension symbolically marks the encroachment of ritual time (or "everywhen") into Christian historical time. Again, the moment of Old Ben's death—the destruction of the incorruptible by corruptible man—and the discovery of his grandfather's immorality occur approximately at the same time in our calendar-world: he is sixteen. His society's participation in the deaths of his spiritual father, Sam Fathers, and of the totem animal, who is his ancestor, is but another manifestation of original sin, like slavery and incest.[19] When

[17] Bellah, *op. cit.*, p. 370.
[18] *Ibid.*
[19] Note that Faulkner makes the sexual act the ritual defining historical and modern religious society. Like the hunt it involves a "no-time," but unlike the hunt "it was like nothing he had ever dreamed." It is this ritual one rejects when he refuses his wife's demands; it is this ritual that links him to his real progenitor

at twenty-one he relinquishes his land, he not only repudiates his culture's depravity; he emotionally substitutes one religion for another. He denies the religion of sin and individual salvation through grace because of the very corruption that it posits and assumes, too late in the movement of history, one that promises unity among all natural things.

To insist that Ike and Santiago are like Christ or Adam before the Fall, to insist upon their innocence, is to falsify the facts of the novels: neither is finally innocent. Both undergo ritual acts that separate them from their routine experience, that provide them with the special knowledge to cope with their situation. Santiago's ritual allows him to assent to his suffering, as he does to the marlin's, to anticipate with resignation the transformation from life to death; Ike's participation in what may seem like a game but which is really a ritual reenactment results in knowledge that causes him to reject the self that is based on a belief in man's flawed nature, in order to identify himself completely with those who are incorruptible because they do not accept a Christian ontology. Faulkner's impulse to make Ike a carpenter, like Christ, is fortunately, not pursued. At no other point is Ike equated with Christ. Neither do Santiago and Ike reveal essentially American material. Each's story manifests, not Western, but primitive religious action and structure. The animal that each faces is local, but what is indigenous is imbedded in a motif that appears in most oral traditions unencumbered by European sophistication.

Carothers McCaslin. Not Christ-like purity, but identification with Sam best explains his celibacy.

A Ritual of Transfiguration:
The Old Man and the Sea

by Arvin R. Wells

The Old Man and the Sea develops a familiar Hemingway theme—the theme of the undefeated. Like other Hemingway treatments of the same theme, this one presents the story of a moral triumph which has as its absolutely necessary condition an apparently smashing defeat. The literary lineage of the old fisherman himself goes back to several Hemingway "code heroes," and, as Philip Young observed,

> Particularly he is related to men like . . . Manuel Garcia, "The Undefeated" bullfighter, who lose[s], in one way, but win[s] in another. Like Manuel, Santiago is a fighter whose best days are behind him and, worse, is wholly down on his luck. But he still dares, and sticks to the rules, and will not quit when he is licked. He is undefeated, he endures, and his loss, therefore, in the manner of it, is itself a victory.[1]

This, in effect, is what it means to be a Hemingway "code hero," but the manner of Santiago's loss and of Hemingway's presentation of it is such that it sets the old fisherman apart from all predecessors. He is the apotheosis of the code hero; his experience is not only a confirmation of personal dignity and courage but what is perhaps best called a ritual of transfiguration.

The sense of ritual accompanies the whole action from the opening dialogues between Santiago and Manolin, in which ritualized questions and responses serve to sustain an innocent illusion of uncompromised respect and dignity, to the final disposal of the remains of the great fish. This sense of ritual action is fostered by the simplicity of the style, by verbal repetition, by the deliberateness with which even small acts are performed, and by the old fisherman's own sense of

---

"A Ritual of Transfiguration: The Old Man and the Sea" *by Arvin R. Wells. From* The University Review, XXX *(Winter, 1963), 95–101. Copyright © 1963 by the University of Missouri at Kansas City. Reprinted by permission of* The University Review.

[1] Philip Young, *Ernest Hemingway* (Rinehart & Co.: New York, 1952), p. 96.

mystery, and it is re-enforced by what might be called reminiscences of Christianity, present in the story sometimes as symbol, sometimes as direct allusion and sometimes merely as a matter of tone. The transfiguration that is at the heart of the story, however, is no Christian mystery; it is "in the manner of it" fundamentally and essentially pagan.

This is not to say that there isn't something of the Christian saint about Santiago. He has achieved the most difficult and saintly of all Christian virtues, humility, a humility so absolute that it involves "no loss of true pride." [2] There is even in him a suggestion of Saint Francis, in his response to animal life and especially to birds—the "small delicate black terns" and the small warbler that comes to rest on his fishing line. Moreover, at various moments in the story Santiago affirms the major Christian virtues: Faith—" 'He hasn't much faith!' 'No . . . But we have' " (10–11). Hope—"It is silly not to hope, he thought. Besides, I believe it is a sin" (104–05). And charity—the old fisherman's generous, unsentimental love of men and animals. But as the old fisherman moves away from the shore and out into the sea, it becomes apparent that, if in any sense he is or is to become a saint, his sainthood is of a non-Christian order.

His "charity" arises, not from the feeling that all are God's creatures, but from a sense that he and all natural creatures participate in the same pattern of necessity and are subject to the same judgment: " 'Take a good rest, small bird,' he said. 'Then go in and take your chance like any man or bird or fish' " (55). His relation to the sea and to the life of the sea is intensely personal and pagan. The sea is "la mar"; it is feminine, not quite personified, but capable, in a moment of fantasy, of taking a lover beneath a blanket of yellow seaweed. It gives forth life and reabsorbs it: the old man is fascinated by the sight of a dead fish growing smaller and smaller as it sinks.

Moreover, for him the realm of nature and the realm of morality are coexistent; the creatures of the sea express for him all that he knows about life—the falseness of the Portuguese man-of-war, the playfulness of the dolphin, the nobility and endurance of the marlin. If there is a god in Santiago's life (he says he is not religious), it is the sea, and the sea, as traditionally, is life itself, which Santiago both loves and mistrusts but to which he can commit himself because he knows "many tricks" and because he can endure. Though he does not make of them grounds for superiority, he has, nonetheless, his intelligence and his will.

Similarly, Santiago's faith and hope rest, not upon any belief in a

[2] Ernest Hemingway, *The Old Man and the Sea,* The Scribner Library (New York, 1952), p. 14. All future references to *The Old Man and the Sea* are to page numbers in this edition, cited parenthetically in the text.

just and benevolent God, but upon his belief in man's ability to endure suffering. This basis of hope is implicit even in the early pages of the story. When we first see Santiago, he appears immensely old, he has been 84 days without catching a fish, and he carries a sail which, furled, "looked like the flag of permanent defeat" (9). Yet, "his hope and his confidence had never gone" (13); he only needs luck, and in the past he has been lucky. Significantly, the signs of that luck are visible in the old man's hands: "His hands had the deep-creased scars from handling heavy fish on the cords. But none of these scars were fresh. They were as old as erosions in a fishless desert" (10). Clearly, in Santiago's world, luck and pain are closely related. Luck is something that comes and goes, and a man may hope for it from day to day, but it is meaningless unless he can endure pain.

In the first few pages of the story the word "faith" appears twice— once, when the old fisherman affirms that he has faith, and then again later, in a very different context. During a conversation about base-ball, Santiago says to Manolin, "Have faith in the Yankees my son. Think of the great DiMaggio" (17). A bit later this attitude is further elaborated in talk between the boy and the fisherman.

> "In the American league it is the Yankees as I said," the old man said happily.
> "They lost today," the boy told him.
> "That means nothing. The great DiMaggio is himself again."
> "They have other men on the team."
> "Naturally. But he makes the difference." (21)

One can have faith in the Yankees, because DiMaggio makes the dif-ference. In just what way he makes the difference becomes clear only later.

During the long ordeal of his struggle with the great fish and then against the sharks, the old man thinks repeatedly of DiMaggio, won-dering whether or not DiMaggio would approve of the way in which he has fished and endured. Behind this is no merely childlike idoliza-tion of a baseball player. The DiMaggio of these reveries is first of all a man with a mysterious and painful ailment, a bone spur; he is, in other words, a man who performs well against the handicap of pain. And it is this that makes the difference. One can afford to place his faith where he finds the power to endure suffering, and this power Santiago finds in himself and in other men. In the end, for him, pain becomes literally the means of distinguishing reality from unreality— "He had only to look at his hands and feel his back against the stern to know that this had truly happened and was not a dream" (98); and it is all but synonymous with life itself—"He put his two hands to-gether and felt the palms . . . and he could bring the pain of life by simply opening and closing them" (116). The power to endure suffering, then, which is in man, gives the power of mastery over life and thus a basis for hope and faith.

In a sense, *The Old Man and the Sea* is a study in pain, in the endurance of pain and in the value of that endurance. The old fisherman fishes as much for a chance to prove himself as he does for a living, and, though he fails to bring the giant marlin to market, he wins the supreme chance to prove himself in the terms he best understands. Starting in simple physical pain, he transcends, through his agony, his own heroic ideal, personified in DiMaggio, and ends in the attitude of the crucified Christ: "He slept face down on the newspapers with his arms out straight and the palms of his hands up" (122). All this he endures without compromising his code either as man or fisherman; he succeeds in showing "what a man can do and what a man endures" (66).

Hemingway's story, however, does not place a final emphasis upon endurance as a value in itself. Within the pattern of the story, endurance like pain is a necessary condition, not so much of victory but of being "undefeated." The fundamental qualities of the old man's character—his humility, his simple and pagan reverence for the conditions and processes of life, and his capacity for suffering—serve to transform his struggle into something which he himself vaguely feels to be a mystery, and his defeat into a triumph as much as the divinity of Christ transforms the terror and sorrow of the Crucifixion into the promise of life.

Before the old fisherman is himself identified by obvious allusion with the crucified Christ, he is identified with Cain and with the crucifiers of Christ. Once he has hooked the great fish, all of his generalized sense of humble brotherhood with other creatures of the sea concentrates upon this one magnificent marlin. Repeatedly, he addresses the fish as "brother"; the taut line that connects them becomes an expression of an equally strong bond of suffering and, on the fisherman's part, of love. Yet, at the same time, he is relentlessly determined to capture and kill the marlin, as Cain killed his brother and as the Roman soldiers killed Christ. That the great fish is somehow to be associated with Christ is not left to conjecture based on traditional symbolism. " 'Christ,' " Santiago exclaims in wonder. " 'I did not know he was so big.' 'I'll kill him though . . . In all his greatness and his glory' " (66). Significantly this is the only place in the story where the expletive, Christ, is used, and the echo in the second sentence is unmistakable—"for thine is the kingdom and the power and the glory forever." When Santiago does slay the fish, he drives the harpoon into his side below the chest fin, "that rose high in the air to the altitude of the man's chest" (94), and pierces the heart. Then the fish rises into the air and hangs there a moment, and there is "some great strangeness" (98) in it.

The old fisherman is not unaware of the paradox of his situation. He thinks, "It is good that we do not have to try to kill the sun or the moon or the stars. It is enough to live on the sea and kill our true brothers" (75). He thinks on occasion that perhaps he should not have been a fisherman; yet the question is scarcely admissible. He was born to be a fisherman; he is a fisherman of necessity, and he must kill the giant fish out of a necessity that is deeper than hunger.

Santiago is, of course, incapable of articulating just what this necessity is, but the pattern of the story makes it clear enough. All the qualities which Santiago sees in the great fish—beauty, nobility, courage, calmness and endurance—are the qualities which he values most; they are the qualities which *redeem* life from meaninglessness and futility (this is perhaps the fundamental link in the story between the fish and Christ); and they are the qualities that Santiago wishes to confirm in himself. Paradoxically the only means he has of confirming them in himself is by exercising them in opposition to the fish. He must, symbolically, slay the lord of life in order to achieve a spiritual identity with him.

Thus the central event of the story is one in which the redemption of life and the destruction of life, affirmation and guilt, are locked in a single action. While he actually is battling the great fish, there is some thought of injustice but none of guilt in the old man's mind. There is only the bond of love and suffering and the sense of mystery, the sense of some deep necessity that the old man cannot quite bring into consciousness. But after the first shark, the Mako shark, has mutilated the fish, thoughts of sin come to tease the old man's mind. "Perhaps it was a sin to kill the fish. I suppose it was even though I did it to keep me alive and feed many people. But then everything is a sin. . . . everything kills everything else" (105–6).

The old man, who has said he is not religious, cannot quite believe in sin in the orthodox Christian understanding of the word; yet, he cannot evade the sense of sin in connection with his killing of the fish. He has chosen "to go there to find him beyond all people" (50). He may argue, "I did it to keep me alive and feed many people" (105), but he knows, as he confesses, that the boy Manolin keeps him alive, and he has said earlier that no one is worthy to eat of the great fish. Here again in the idea of worthiness with its suggestion of communion, the Christian allusion is clear, but in the context of the story worthiness is something acquired in action, by being great in the same way the fish is great.

The old man cannot resolve the question of guilt for himself; he can only oppose to it his conviction of necessity: "You were born to be

a fisherman as the fish was born to be a fish" (105). And in the fight
against the sharks, the feeling of sin is lost and replaced by something
more congenial to the spirit of the old man, something like the idea
of *hybris*.

> And what beat you? he thought.
> "Nothing," he said aloud. "I went out too far." (120)

While the question of sin and guilt persists, however, the old man tries
to deal with it honestly, and having counseled himself against ration-
alization, he leans forward, almost unconsciously tears a piece of the
flesh from the giant marlin, and eats of the fish of which no one is
worthy to eat.

It is only after this act, which the reader has been prepared to recognize as a kind of communion, that we meet the first of the allusions
that serve to refer the old man's experience to the Passion of Christ.
As he sees the first of the shovel-nose sharks approaching, the old man
utters a cry: "'Ay,' he said aloud." And the reader is told, "There is
no translation for this word and perhaps it is just a noise such as
a man might make, involuntarily, feeling the nail go through his hands
and into the wood" (107).

Before this, all symbols associated with and all allusions made to
Christ's Passion have been applied to the giant fish. Now begins a
process of transfer from the fish to the man. As he leaves the skiff, the
old man falls and lies for a moment with the mast across his shoulders;
he must sit down five times before he reaches his shack on the hill, and
when he reaches the shack, he lies down in the attitude of the crucified
Christ.

The point of this accumulation of allusions is not simply, as Philip
Young has suggested, that life crucifies even the strong and noble in
the end and that the important thing is how one takes it when it
comes. The transfer of Christian symbols and allusions from the great
fish to the fisherman is, in fact, only part, perhaps only the most obvious part, of a fairly complex process through which identity is
established between them.

Santiago fights and kills the great marlin "out of pride," out of the
desire to show that he is like the great fish. What he seeks is identity.
He affirms continually his own feeling of brotherhood, but, in another
sense, brotherhood can be affirmed only in a struggle that must end
in the death of the fish. In a moment of semi-delirium just before he
kills the fish, the old man's sense of identity with him becomes so intense that he thinks, "Never have I seen a greater, or more beautiful,
or a calmer or more noble thing than you, brother. Come on and kill
me. I do not care who kills who" (92).

After the fish is dead the old man has a strong desire to touch him, to confirm the reality of the fish and, thereby, the reality of what he has proven of himself. The delusion of confused identities persists as the old man, seeing the giant carcass of the fish alongside, wonders, "Is he bringing me in or am I bringing him in?" (99). When the fish is hit and mutilated by the first shark, the old fisherman feels "as though he himself were hit" (103). Later, when, without pride, almost unconsciously the old man eats of the fish, the fish becomes a part of his life. Almost immediately the *galanos* approach, and we encounter the first of the allusions that refer the old man's experience to the Passion of Christ. The pattern is extremely tight and neat: just as the great marlin in his noble but futile struggle to preserve his life becomes identified symbolically with the crucified Christ, so the old man in his noble but futile struggle to preserve the fish from the sharks becomes identified with the same figure.

Seen as a part of this general pattern, the fact of crucifixion no longer suggests either, on the one hand, a vague evocation of Christianity or, on the other, merely the supreme experience of "the pain of life" and the supreme test of endurance. It is the final seal of the old man's triumph. Through the tragic image of Christ in his agony, the identity of the fisherman with the fish, that is, with the essentially pagan virtues which the fish represents, is finally affirmed. The justification for this non-Christian use of Christian symbolism stems not only from the fact that the giant marlin expresses in action all those qualities that, for the old man, redeem life, but from the fact that the Crucifixion is a consummate metaphor for the medium of suffering, endurance, and apparent defeat through which the old man achieves his at least momentary transfiguration.

When the old man reaches shore he has only the skeleton of the marlin. The experience has been stripped of its practical and material aspects, and even the great skeleton is at last only so much more garbage waiting to go out with the tide. At most it serves to give the other fishermen a clue as to what the struggle must have been; to the outsiders, the man and woman tourists who look down from the terrace, it is all but meaningless. They perceive some strange beauty in the thing itself, but they cannot distinguish even the elementary terms of the experience.

> "I didn't know sharks had such handsome, beautifully formed tails."
> "I didn't either," her male companion said. (127)

Having lost his fish to the least worthy of opponents, the shovel-nose sharks that are just moving appetites, even the old man is unclear about what he has accomplished, and the boy, Manolin, whose admiration and pity counterpoint the old man's humility, must order the experience for him.

"They beat me, Manolin," he said. "They truly beat me."
"*He* didn't beat you. Not the fish."
"No. Truly. It was afterwards." (124)

Finally the old fisherman seems almost indifferent to the great struggle; he is beyond it; it is complete in itself, and the others may take from it what they can: the head of the marlin to Pedrico, the spear to Manolin, the uncomprehending glimpse of the skeleton to the two tourists. But the gap between what the experience has actually been and what the others can gather from the remains is strongly suggested by the total lack of connection between their concern with the skeleton and the dream of the lions which fills the old man's sleep at the close of the story.

In a sense, the old man's final reward for having endured is the freedom which he finally has to dream, uninterrupted, of the lions that he had once seen playing like cats upon the shores of Africa and that somehow now are "the main thing that is left" (66). The dream has come before during the story, but always before the old man was called back to a reality of further action and further suffering. Now, that reality is held at a distance. For the old man there is a childlike happiness and reassurance in seeing the great beasts at play. What the lions represent beyond this is broadly suggested by the details of the dream in their relation to the general pattern of action and symbol.

The lions, traditionally, are the noblest of the great beasts in comparison with which man, according to the old fisherman, "is not much." They are the kings of the jungle, primal nature, which they dominate by their courage, their strength, their fierceness and their supposed pride. They are both like and unlike the great marlin: like him in that they have the qualities that redeem life and are in this way the lords of life; unlike him in that their beauty and nobility are compounded with fierceness and therefore inspire not only awe but fear. In the dream, however, the lions come out from the jungle and down onto the beach to play on the sand; they have put aside their majesty and have grown domestic and familiar. It is as if they gave themselves up to the old man, to his love, without the necessity of further trial or guilt or suffering.

As the lions come out of the jungle and fill the old man's sleep, their cat-like playfulness, free of threat or challenge, suggests a harmony between the old man and the heroic qualities which the lions possess and the giant marlin possessed and which the old man has fought to realize in himself. Most simply, perhaps, they suggest an achieved intimacy between the old man and the proud and often fierce heart of nature that for him is the repository of values.

The Heroic Impulse in
The Old Man and the Sea

by Leo Gurko

Most of Hemingway's novels emphasize what men cannot do, and define the world's limitations, cruelties, or built-in evil. *The Old Man and the Sea* is remarkable for its stress on what men can do and on the world as an arena where heroic deeds are possible. The universe inhabited by Santiago, the old Cuban fisherman, is not free of tragedy and pain but these are transcended, and the affirming tone is in sharp contrast with the pessimism permeating such books as *The Sun Also Rises* and *A Farewell to Arms.*

One aspect of this universe, familiar from the earlier works, is its changelessness. The round of Nature—which includes human nature —is not only eternal but eternally the same. The sun not only rises, it rises always, and sets and rises again without change of rhythm. The relationship of Nature to man proceeds through basic patterns that never vary. Therefore, despite the fact that a story by Hemingway is always full of action, the action takes place inside a world that is fundamentally static.

Moreover, its processes are purely secular in character: Hemingway's figures are often religious but their religion is peripheral rather than central to their lives. In *The Old Man and the Sea,* Santiago, the principal figure, is a primitive Cuban, at once religious and superstitious. Yet neither his religion nor his superstitious beliefs are relevant to his tragic experience with the great marlin; they do not create it or in any way control its meaning. The fisherman himself, knowing what it is all about, relies on his own resources and not on God (in whom he devoutly believes, just as Jake Barnes, while calling himself a bad Catholic, is also a devout believer). If he succeeds in catching the fish, he "will say ten Our Fathers and ten Hail Marys . . . and make a

"The Heroic Impulse in The Old Man and the Sea" *by Leo Gurko. From* English Journal, *XLIV* (*October, 1955*), *377–82.* (*The same article appears under the title* "The Old Man and the Sea" *in* College English, *XVII* (*October, 1955*), *11–15.*) *Copyright 1955 by the National Council of Teachers of English. Reprinted by permission of the National Council of Teachers of English and Leo Gurko.*

pilgrimage to the Virgen de Cobre," but these are rituals that come after the event and have no significant relationship with it.

In this universe, changeless and bare of divinity, everyone has his fixed role to play. Santiago's role is to pursue the great marlin, "That which I was born for," he reflects; the marlin's is to live in the deepest parts of the sea and escape the pursuit of man. The two of them struggle with each other to the death, but without animosity or hatred. On the contrary, the old man feels a deep affection and admiration for the fish. He admires its great strength as it pulls his skiff out to sea, and becomes conscious of its nobility as the two grow closer and closer together, in spirit as well as space, during their long interlude on the Gulf Stream. In the final struggle between them, his hands bleeding, his body racked with fatigue and pain, the old man reflects in his exhaustion:

> You are killing me, fish. . . . But you have a right to. Never have I seen a greater, or more beautiful, or a calmer or a more noble thing than you, brother. Come on and kill me. I do not care who kills who.

On the homeward journey, with the marlin tied to the boat and already under attack from sharks, Santiago establishes his final relationship with the fish, that great phenomenon of Nature:

> You did not kill the fish only to keep alive and to sell for food, he thought. You killed him for pride and because you are a fisherman. You loved him when he was alive and you loved him after. If you love him, it is not a sin to kill him.

A sense of brotherhood and love, in a world in which everyone is killing or being killed, binds together the creatures of Nature, establishes between them a unity and an emotion which transcends the destructive pattern in which they are caught. In the eternal round, each living thing, man and animal, acts out its destiny according to the drives of its species, and in the process becomes a part of the profound harmony of the natural universe. This harmony, taking into account the hard facts of pursuit, violence, and death but reaching a stage of feeling beyond them, is a primary aspect of Hemingway's view of the world. Even the sharks have their place. They are largely scavengers, but the strongest and most powerful among them, the great Mako shark which makes its way out of the deep part of the sea, shares the grandeur of the marlin. Santiago kills him but feels identified with him as well:

> But you enjoyed killing the *dentuso,* he thought. He lives on the live fish as you do. He is not a scavenger nor just a moving appetite as some sharks are. He is beautiful and noble and knows no fear of anything.

Nature not only has its own harmony and integration but also its degrees of value. In *The Old Man and the Sea* this is contained in the idea of depth. The deeper the sea the more valuable the creatures living there and the more intense the experience deriving from it. On the day that he catches the great marlin, the old man goes much farther out than the other fishermen and casts bait in much deeper water. The marlin itself is a denizen of the profounder depths. Even the Mako shark lives in the deep water and its speed, power, and directness are qualities associated with depth. There are, in fact, two orders in every species: the great marlins and the lesser, the great sharks and the smaller, bad-smelling, purely scavenger sharks who dwell in shallower water and attack with a sly indirectness in demeaning contrast with the bold approach of the Mako. There are also two kinds of men—as there have always been in Hemingway—the greater men and the lesser, heroes and ordinary humans.

To be a hero means to dare more than other men, to expose oneself to greater dangers, and therefore more greatly to risk the possibilities of defeat and death. On the eighty-fifth day after catching his last fish, Santiago rows far beyond the customary fishing grounds; as he drops his lines into water of unplumbed depth he sees the other fishermen, looking very small, strung out in a line far inland between himself and the shore. Because he is out so far, he catches the great fish. But because the fish is so powerful, it pulls his skiff even farther out—so far from shore then that they cannot get back in time to prevent the marlin being chewed to pieces by the sharks.

> "I shouldn't have gone out so far, fish," he said. "Neither for you nor for me. I'm sorry, fish."

The greatness of the experience and the inevitability of the loss are bound up together. Nature provides us with boundless opportunities for the great experience if we have it in us to respond. The experience carries with it its heavy tragic price. No matter. It is worth it. When Santiago at last returns with the marlin still lashed to the skiff but eaten away to the skeleton, he staggers uphill to his hut groaning under the weight of the mast. He falls asleep exhausted and dreams of the African lions he had seen in his younger days at sea. The next morning the other fishermen gaze in awe at the size of the skeleton, measure it to see by how much it is recordbreaking, while the reverential feeling of the boy, Manolin, for the fisherman is strongly reenforced. Everyone has somehow been uplifted by the experience. Even on the lowest, most ignorant level, it creates a sensation. The tourists in the last scene of the story mistake the marlin for a shark but they too are struck by a sense of the extraordinary.

The world not only contains the possibilities of heroic adventure and emotion to which everyone, on whatever level, can respond, but it also has continuity. Santiago is very old and has not much time left. But he has been training Manolin to pick up where he leaves off. The boy has been removed by his parents from the old man's boat because of his bad luck, but this in no way diminishes the boy's eagerness to be like Santiago. The master-pupil relationship between them suggests that the heroic impulse is part of a traditional process handed down from one generation to another, that the world is a continuous skein of possibility and affirmation. This affirming note, subdued in Hemingway's earlier fiction, is sounded here with unambiguous and unrestricted clarity.

Indeed, Santiago is the clearest representation of the hero because he is the only major character in Hemingway who has not been permanently wounded or disillusioned. His heroic side is suggested throughout. Once, in Casablanca, he defeated a huge Negro from Cienfuegos at the hand game and was referred to thereafter as *El Campéon*. Now in his old age, he is hero-worshipped by Manolin who wants always to fish with him, or, when he cannot, at least to help him even with his most menial chores. At sea Santiago, sharing the Cuban craze for baseball, thinks frequently of Joe DiMaggio, the greatest ballplayer of his generation, and wonders whether DiMaggio, suffering from a bone spur in his heel, ever endured the pain which the marlin is now subjecting him to. And at night, when he sleeps, he dreams of lions playing on the beaches of Africa. The constant association with the king of ballplayers and the king of beasts adds to the old man's heroic proportions. He is heroic even in his bad luck. The story opens with the announcement that he has gone eighty-four days without taking a fish—ordinary men are seldom afflicted with disaster so outsized.

Heightening and intensifying these already magnified effects is the extraordinary beauty of Nature which cozens and bemuses us with its sensuous intoxications. The account of the sea coming to life at dawn is one of the most moving passages in the story, supplemented later at rhapsodic intervals by the drama of the great pursuit. This comes to its visual climax with the first great jump of the marlin when, for the first time, Santiago sees the gigantic size of his prey. Hemingway pays very close attention to the rippling and fluting of the water, to wind currents, the movements of turtles, fish, and birds, the rising of sun and stars. One is filled not simply with a sense of Nature's vastness, but of her enchantment. This enchantment adds an aesthetic dimension to Santiago's adventure, an adventure whose heroism invests it with moral meaning and whose invocation of comradeship and identity supply it with emotional grandeur.

Within this universe, where there is no limit to the depth of experience, learning how to function is of the greatest importance. It is not enough to have will; one must also have technique. If will is what enables one to live, technique is what enables one to live successfully. Santiago is not a journeyman fisherman, but a superb craftsman who knows his business thoroughly and always practices it with great skill. He keeps his lines straight where others allow them to drift with the current. "It is better to be lucky," he thinks. "But I would rather be exact. Then when luck comes you are ready." To be ready—with all one's professional as well as psychological resources—that is the imperative. One reason that Hemingway's stories are so crammed with technical details about fishing, hunting, bull-fighting, boxing, and war —so much so that they often read like manuals on these subjects—is his belief that professional technique is the quickest and surest way of understanding the physical processes of Nature, of getting into the thing itself. Men should study the world in which they are born as the most serious of all subjects; they can live in it only as they succeed in handling themselves with skill. Life is more than an endurance contest. It is also an art, with rules, rituals, and methods that, once learned, lead on to mastery.

Furthermore, when the great trial comes, one must be alone. The pressure and the agony cannot be shared or sloughed off on others, but must be endured alone. Santiago, his hands chafed and bleeding from the pull of the marlin, his face cut, in a state of virtual prostration from his struggle, several times wishes the boy were with him to ease the strain, but it is essential that he go unaccompanied, that in the end he rely on his own resources and endure his trial unaided. At the bottom of this necessity for solitariness, there is the incurable reliance on the individual which makes Hemingway the great contemporary inheritor of the romantic tradition. The stripping down of existence to the struggle between individual man and the natural world, during the course of which he rises to the highest levels of himself, has an early echo in Keats's line "Then on the shore of the wide world I stand alone. . . ." In modern fiction it is Melville and Conrad who give this theme its most significant shape. The mysterious, inscrutable, dramatic Nature into which their heroes plunge themselves in search of their own self-realization supplies Hemingway with the scaffolding for *The Old Man and the Sea*. Like Captain Ahab, like Lord Jim, Santiago is pitched into the dangerous ocean; for only there, and with only himself to fall back on, can he work out his destiny and come to final terms with life.

The concept of the hero whose triumph consists of stretching his own powers to their absolute limits regardless of the physical results gives *The Old Man and the Sea* a special place among its author's works. It confronts us with a man who is not only capable of making the ultimate effort, but makes it successfully and continuously. This theme of affirmation, that had begun to be struck in *Across the River and into the Trees,* is present here much more convincingly. Colonel Cantwell of the immediately preceding novel is forever talking about his heroism; Santiago acts his out. Cantwell reminisces on past triumphs; the old fisherman demonstrates them before our eyes. The strain of boastful exhibitionism that causes some readers to regard Hemingway as an adolescent Byron spoiled Cantwell's story. It is almost totally absent from Santiago's.

Here we have entered a world which has to some degree recovered from the gaping wounds that made it so frightening a place in the early stories. The world which injured Jake Barnes so cruelly, pointlessly deprived Lieutenant Henry of his one love, destroyed Harry Morgan at the height of his powers, and robbed Robert Jordan of his political idealism has now begun to regain its balance. It is no longer the bleak trap within which man is doomed to struggle, suffer, and die as bravely as he can, but a meaningful, integrated structure that challenges our resources, holds forth rich emotional rewards for those who live in it daringly and boldly though continuing to exact heavy payment from them in direct proportion to how far they reach out. There is no less tragedy than before, but this has lost its bleakness and accidentality, and become purposive. It is this sense of purposiveness that makes its first appearance in Hemingway's philosophy, and sets off *The Old Man and the Sea* from his other fiction.

After the first World War the traditional hero disappeared from Western literature, to be replaced in one form or another by Kafka's Mr. K. Hemingway's protagonists, from Nick Adams on, were hemmed in like Mr. K. by a bewildering cosmos which held them in a tight vise. The huge complicated mushrooming of politics, society, and the factory age began to smother freedom of action on the individual's part. In his own life Hemingway tended to avoid the industrialized countries including his own, and was drawn from the start to the primitive places of Spain, Africa, and Cuba. For there, the ancient struggle and harmony between man and Nature still existed, and the heroic possibilities so attractive to Hemingway's temperament had freer play. At last, in the drama of Santiago, a drama entirely outside the framework of modern society and its institutions, he was able to bring these possibilities to their first full fruition, and re-discover, in however specialized a context, the hero lost in the twentieth century.

Thus *The Old Man and the Sea* is the culmination of Hemingway's long search for disengagement from the social world and total entry into the natural. This emerges in clearer focus than ever before as one of the major themes in his career both as writer and man. Jake and Bill are happy only in the remote countryside outside Burguete, away from the machinery of postwar Europe. It is when Lieutenant Henry signs his separate peace, deserts from the Italian army, and retires with his love to the high Swiss mountains far removed from the man-made butchery of the war that he enjoys his brief moment of unclouded bliss. The defeated writer in "The Snows of Kilimanjaro," as he lies dying, laments his inability to free himself from the complicated temptations of money, fashion, the life of sophisticated dilettantism, and thinks of his lost talent as resting unspoiled on the remote virginal snows cresting the summit of an African mountain (height on land is plainly the moral equivalent in Hemingway to depth in the sea). Robert Jordan must first disengage himself from the political machinery of Spain before the act of sacrificing his life for his comrades can acquire its note of pure spiritual exaltation.

The movement to get out of society and its artifices is not motivated by the desire to escape but by the desire for liberation. Hemingway seeks to immerse himself totally in Nature not to "evade his responsibilities" but to free his moral and emotional self. Since life in society is necessarily stunting and artificial, cowardice consists not of breaking out of it but of continuing in it. To be true to oneself makes a return to the lost world of Nature categorically imperative. And that lost world, as *The Old Man and the Sea* reveals, has its own responsibilities, disciplines, moralities, and all-embracing meaning quite the equivalent of anything present in society and of much greater value because it makes possible a total response to the demands upon the self. Santiago is the first of the main figures in Hemingway who is not an American, and who is altogether free of the entanglements of modern life. It is toward the creation of such a figure that Hemingway has been moving, however obscurely, from the beginning. His ability to get inside this type of character without the fatal self-consciousness that mars so much literary "primitivism" is a measure of how far he has succeeded, in imagination at least, in freeing himself from the familiar restraints of convention.

In this movement from the confinements of society to the challenges of Nature, Hemingway is most closely linked to Conrad. Conrad thrust his Europeans into the pressures of the Malayan archipelago and darkest Africa because he was convinced that only when removed from the comforts and protective mechanisms of civilization could they be put to the test. In his one London novel, *The Secret Agent,* Conrad demonstrated that suffering and tragedy were as possible in Brixton and Camberwell as off the Java coast; heroism, however, was not, and *The Secret Agent* stands as his one major work that remained hero-less. This embracing of Nature has nothing of Rousseau in it; it is not a revulsion against the corruption and iniquity of urban life. It is, instead, a flight from safety and the atrophying of the spirit produced by safety.

It is for the sake of the liberation of the human spirit rather than the purification of social institutions that Conrad and Hemingway play out their lonely dramas in the bosom of Nature.

Because *The Old Man and the Sea* records this drama in its most successful form, it gives off in atmosphere and tone a buoyant sense of release that is new in Hemingway. The story, then, may well be less a capstone of Hemingway's extraordinary career to date than a fresh emotional point of departure for the work to come.

The Old Man and the Sea:
Hemingway's Tragic Vision of Man

by Clinton S. Burhans, Jr.

I

In *Death in the Afternoon,* Hemingway uses an effective metaphor to describe the kind of prose he is trying to write: he explains that "if a writer of prose knows enough about what he is writing about he may omit things that he knows and the reader, if the writer is writing truly enough, will have a feeling of those things as strongly as though the writer had stated them. The dignity of movement of an iceberg is due to only one-eighth of it being above water." [1]

Among all the works of Hemingway which illustrate this metaphor, none, I think, does so more consistently or more thoroughly than the saga of Santiago. Indeed, the critical reception of the novel has emphasized this aspect of it: in particular, Philip Young, Leo Gurko, and Carlos Baker have stressed the qualities of *The Old Man and the Sea* as allegory and parable. [2] Each of these critics is especially concerned with two qualities in Santiago—his epic individualism and the love he feels for the creatures who share with him a world of inescapable violence—though in the main each views these qualities from a different point of the literary compass. Young regards the novel as essentially classical in nature; [3] Gurko sees it as reflecting Hemingway's romanticism; [4] and to Baker, the novel is Christian in context, and the old fisherman is suggestive of Christ. [5]

---

[1] Ernest Hemingway, *Death in the Afternoon* (New York, 1932), p. 183.

[2] On the other hand—though not, to me, convincingly—Otto Friedrich, "Ernest Hemingway: Joy Through Strength," *The American Scholar,* XXVI (Autumn, 1957), 470, 513–30 sees Santiago's experience as little more than the result of the necessities of his profession.

[3] Philip Young, *Hemingway* (New York, 1952), p. 100.

[4] Leo Gurko, "The Old Man and the Sea," *College English,* XVII (Oct., 1955), I, 14.

[5] Carlos Baker, *Hemingway* (Princeton, 1956), p. 299.

Such interpretations of *The Old Man and the Sea* are not, of course, contradictory; in fact, they are parallel at many points. All are true, and together they point to both the breadth and depth of the novel's enduring significance and also to its central greatness: like all great works of art it is a mirror wherein every man perceives a personal likeness. Such viewpoints, then, differ only in emphasis and reflect generally similar conclusions—that Santiago represents a noble and tragic individualism revealing what man can do in an indifferent universe which defeats him, and the love he can feel for such a universe and his humility before it.

True as this is, there yet remains, I think, a deeper level of significance, a deeper level upon which the ultimate beauty and the dignity of movement of this brilliant structure fundamentally rest. On this level of significance, Santiago is Harry Morgan alive again and grown old; for what comes to Morgan in a sudden and unexpected revelation as he lies dying is the matrix of the old fisherman's climactic experience. Since 1937, Hemingway has been increasingly concerned with the relationship between individualism and interdependence;[6] and *The Old Man and the Sea* is the culminating expression of this concern in its reflection of Hemingway's mature view of the tragic irony of man's fate: that no abstraction can bring man an awareness and understanding of the solidarity and interdependence without which life is impossible; he must learn it, as it has always been truly learned, through the agony of active and isolated individualism in a universe which dooms such individualism.

II

Throughout *The Old Man and the Sea*, Santiago is given heroic proportions. He is "a strange old man," [7] still powerful and still wise

[6] This direction in Hemingway's thought and art has, of course, been pointed out by several critics, particularly by Edgar Johnson in the *Sewanee Review*, XLVIII (July–Sept., 1940), 3 and by Maxwell Geismar in *Writers in Crisis* (Cambridge, Mass., 1942). With prophetic insight, Johnson says that "the important thing about Hemingway is that he has earned his philosophy, that he has struggled to reach it, overcome the obstacles to attaining it. . . . He has earned the right to reject rejection. For the good, the gentle and the brave, he now tells us, if they do not try to stand alone and make a separate peace, defeat is not inevitable. His life-blood dripping into the bottom of the boat, Harry Morgan realized it at the end of his career. Philip Rawlings realized it in the blood and terror and tragedy and splendor even of a dying Madrid. Hemingway has realized it there too, and the realization may well be for him the very beginning of a new and more vital career."

[7] Ernest Hemingway, *The Old Man and the Sea*, The Scribner Library (New York, 1952), p. 14.

in all the ways of his trade. After he hooks the great marlin, he fights him with epic skill and endurance, showing "what a man can do and what a man endures" (p. 66). And when the sharks come, he is determined to " 'fight them until I die' " (p. 115), because he knows that " 'man is not made for defeat. . . . A man can be destroyed but not defeated' " (p. 103).

In searching for and in catching his big fish, Santiago gains a deepened insight into himself and into his relationship to the rest of created life—an insight as pervasive and implicit in the old fisherman's experience as it is sudden and explicit in Harry Morgan's. As he sails far out on the sea, Santiago thinks of it "as feminine and as something that gave or withheld great favours, and if she did wild or wicked things it was because she could not help them" (p. 30). For the bird who rests on his line and for other creatures who share with him such a capricious and violent life, the old man feels friendship and love (pp. 29, 48). And when he sees a flight of wild ducks go over, the old man knows "no man was ever alone on the sea" (p. 61).

Santiago comes to feel his deepest love for the creature that he himself hunts and kills, the great fish which he must catch not alone for physical need but even more for his pride and his profession. The great marlin is unlike the other fish which the old man catches; he is a spiritual more than a physical necessity. He is unlike the other fish, too, in that he is a worthy antagonist for the old man, and during his long ordeal, Santiago comes to pity the marlin and then to respect and to love him. In the end he senses that there can be no victory for either in the equal struggle between them, that the conditions which have brought them together have made them one (p. 92). And so, though he kills the great fish, the old man has come to love him as his equal and his brother; sharing a life which is a capricious mixture of incredible beauty and deadly violence and in which all creatures are both hunter and hunted, they are bound together in its most primal relationship.

Beyond the heroic individualism of Santiago's struggle with the great fish and his fight against the sharks, however, and beyond the love and the brotherhood which he comes to feel for the noble creature he must kill, there is a further dimension in the old man's experience which gives to these their ultimate significance. For in killing the great marlin and in losing him to the sharks, the old man learns the sin into which men inevitably fall by going far out beyond their depth, beyond their true place in life. In the first night of his struggle with the great fish, the old man begins to feel a loneliness and a sense almost of guilt for the way in which he has caught him (p. 50); and after he has killed the marlin, he feels no pride of accomplishment, no sense of victory. Rather, he seems to feel almost as though he has betrayed the great fish; "I am only better than him through trickery," he thinks, "and he meant me no harm" (p. 99).

Thus, when the sharks come, it is almost as a thing expected, almost as a punishment which the old man brings upon himself in going far out "beyond all people. Beyond all people in the world" (p. 50) and there hooking and killing the great fish. For the coming of the sharks is not a matter of chance nor a stroke of bad luck; "the shark was not an accident" (p. 100). They are the direct result of the old man's action in killing the fish. He has driven his harpoon deep into the marlin's heart, and the blood of the great fish, welling from his heart, leaves a trail of scent which the first shark follows. He tears huge pieces from the marlin's body, causing more blood to seep into the sea and thus attract other sharks; and in killing the first shark, the old man loses his principal weapon, his harpoon. Thus, in winning his struggle with the marlin and in killing him, the old man sets in motion the sequence of events which take from him the great fish whom he has come to love and with whom he identifies himself completely. And the old man senses an inevitability in the coming of the sharks (p. 101), a feeling of guilt which deepens into remorse and regret. "I am sorry that I killed the fish . . ." (p. 103), he thinks, and he tells himself that "You did not kill the fish only to keep alive and to sell for food. . . . You killed him for pride and because you are a fisherman" (p. 105).

Earlier, before he had killed the marlin, Santiago had been " 'glad we do not have to try to kill the stars' " (p. 75). It is enough, he had felt, to have to kill our fellow creatures. Now, with the inevitable sharks attacking, the old man senses that in going far out he has in effect tried "to kill the sun or the moon or the stars." For him it has not been "enough to live on the sea and kill our true brothers"; in his individualism and his need and his pride, he has gone far out "beyond all people," beyond his true place in a capricious and indifferent world, and has thereby brought not only on himself but also on the great fish the forces of violence and destruction. " 'I shouldn't have gone out so far, fish . . . ,' " he declares. " 'Neither for you nor for me. I'm sorry, fish' " (p. 110). And when the sharks have torn away half of the great marlin, Santiago speaks again to his brother in the sea: " 'Half-fish,' he said. 'Fish that you were. I am sorry that I went too far out. I ruined us both' " (p. 115).

The old man's realization of what he has done is reflected in his apologies to the fish, and this realization and its implications are emphasized symbolically throughout the novel. From beginning to end, the theme of solidarity and interdependence pervades the action and provides the structural framework within which the old man's heroic individualism and his love for his fellow creatures appear and function and which gives them their ultimate significance. Having gone eighty-four days without a catch, Santiago has become dependent upon the young boy, Manolin, and upon his other friends in his village. The boy keeps up his confidence and hope, brings him clothes and such necessities as water and soap, and sees that he has fresh bait for his fishing. Martin, the restaurant owner, sends the old man food, and Perico, the wineshop owner, gives him newspapers so that he can read about baseball. All of this the old man accepts gratefully and without shame, knowing that such help is not demeaning. "He was too simple to wonder when he had attained humility. But he knew he had attained it and he knew it was not disgraceful and it carried no loss of true pride" (pp. 13–14).

Santiago refuses the young boy's offer to leave the boat his parents have made him go in and return to his, but soon after he hooks the great marlin he wishes increasingly and often that the boy were with him. And after the sharks come and he wonders if it had been a sin to kill the great fish, the old man thinks that, after all, "everything kills everything else in some way. Fishing kills me exactly as it keeps me alive." But then he remembers that it is not fishing but the love and care of another human being that keeps him alive now; "the boy keeps me alive, he thought. I must not deceive myself too much" (p. 106).

As the sharks tear from him more and more of the great fish and as the boat gets closer to his home, the old man's sense of his relationship to his friends and to the boy deepens: "I cannot be too far out now, he thought. I hope no one has been too worried. There is only the boy to worry, of course. But I am sure he would have confidence. Many of the older fishermen will worry. Many others too, he thought. I live in a good town" (p. 115). In the end, when he awakens in his shack and talks with the boy, he notices "how pleasant it was to have someone to talk to instead of speaking only to himself and to the sea" (p. 124). This time he accepts without any real opposition the boy's insistence on returning to his boat, and he says no more about going far out alone.

This theme of human solidarity and interdependence is reinforced by several symbols. Baseball, which the old man knows well and loves and which he thinks and talks about constantly, is, of course, a highly developed team sport and one that contrasts importantly in this respect with the relatively far more individualistic bullfighting, hunting, and fishing usually found in Hemingway's stories. Although he tells himself that "now is no time to think of baseball" (p. 40), the game is in Santiago's thoughts throughout his ordeal, and he wonders about each day's results in the *Gran Ligas*.

Even more significant is the old man's hero-worship of Joe DiMaggio, the great Yankee outfielder. DiMaggio, like Santiago, was a champion, a master of his craft, and in baseball terms an old one, playing out the last years of his glorious career severely handicapped by the pain of a bone spur in his heel. The image of DiMaggio is a constant source of inspiration to Santiago; in his strained back and his cut and cramped left hand he, too, is an old champion who must endure the handicap of pain; and he tells himself that he "must have confidence and . . . be worthy of the great DiMaggio who does all things perfectly even with the pain of the bone spur in his heel" (p. 68).

But DiMaggio had qualities at least as vital to the Yankees as his courage and individual brilliance. Even during his own time and since then, many men with expert knowledge of baseball have considered other contemporary outfielders—especially Ted Williams of the Boston Red Sox—to be DiMaggio's equal or superior in terms of individual ability and achievement. But few men have ever earned the affection and the renown which DiMaggio received as a "team player"—one who always displayed his individual greatness as part of his team, one to whom the team was always more important than himself. It used to be said of DiMaggio's value as a "team player" that with him in the line-up, even when he was handicapped by the pain in his heel, the Yankees were two runs ahead when they came out on the field. From Santiago's love of baseball and his evident knowledge of it, it is clear that he would be aware of these qualities in DiMaggio. And when Manolin remarks that there are other men on the New York team, the old man replies: " 'Naturally. But he makes the difference' " (p. 21).

The lions which Santiago dreams about and his description in terms of Christ symbols further suggest solidarity and love and humility as opposed to isolated individualism and pride. So evocative and lovely a symbol is the dream of the lions that it would be foolish if not impossible to attempt its literal definition. Yet it seems significant that the old man dreams not of a single lion, a "king of the beasts," a lion proud and powerful and alone, like the one from which Francis Macomber runs in terror, but of several young lions who come down to a beach in the evening to play together. "He only dreamed of places now and of the lions on the beach. They played like young cats in the dusk and he loved them as he loved the boy" (p. 25). It seems also significant that the old man "no longer dreamed of storms, nor of women, nor of great occurrences, nor of great fish, nor fights, nor contests of strength, nor of his wife" (p. 25)—that is that he no longer dreams of great individualistic deeds like the one which brings violence and destruction on him and on the marlin. Instead, the lions are "the main thing that is left" (p. 66), and they evoke the solidarity and love and peace to which the old man returns after hunting and killing and losing his great fish.

These qualities are further emphasized by the symbolic value of the old fisherman as he carries the mast crosslike up the hill to his shack and as he lies exhausted on his bed. His hands have been terribly wounded in catching the great marlin and in fighting the sharks, and as he lies sleeping "face down on the newspapers with his arms out straight and the palms of his hands up" (p. 122), his figure is Christ-like and suggests that if the old man has been crucified by the forces of a capricious and violent universe, the meaning of his experience is the humility and love of Christ and the interdependence which they imply.

Such, then, are the qualities which define man's true place in a world of violence and death indifferent to him, and they are the context which gives the experience of the old fisherman its ultimate significance as the reflection of Hemingway's culminating concept of the human condition—his tragic vision of man. For in his under-standing that "it is enough to live on the sea and kill our true brothers," the fellow creatures who share life with us and whom he loves, the old man is expressing Hemingway's conviction that despite the tragic necessity of such a condition, man has a place in the world. And in his realization that in going alone and too far out, "beyond all people in the world," he has ruined both himself and also the great fish, the old man reflects Hemingway's feeling that in his individualism and his pride and his need, man inevitably goes beyond his true place in the world and thereby brings violence and destruction on himself and on others. Yet in going out too far and alone, Santiago has found his greatest strength and courage and dignity and nobility and love, and in this he expresses Hemingway's view of the ultimate tragic irony of man's fate: that only through the isolated individualism and the pride which drive him beyond his true place in life does man develop the qualities and the wisdom which teach him the sin of such individual-ism and pride and which bring him the deepest understanding of himself and of his place in the world. Thus, in accepting his world for what it is and in learning to live in it, Hemingway has achieved a tragic but ennobling vision of man which is in the tradition of Sopho-cles, Christ, Melville, and Conrad.

III

It is not enough, then, to point out, as Robert P. Weeks does, that "from the first eight words of *The Old Man and the Sea* . . . we are squarely confronted with a world in which man's isolation is the most insistent truth." [8] True as this is, it is truth which is at the same time

    [8] Robert P. Weeks, "Hemingway and the Uses of Isolation," *University of Kansas City Review*, XXIV (Winter, 1957), 125.

paradox, for Santiago is profoundly aware that "no man was ever alone on the sea." Nor is the novel solely what Leo Gurko feels it is—"the culmination of Hemingway's long search for disengagement from the social world and total entry into the natural" (p. 15). If the old man leaves society to go "far out" and "beyond all people in the world," the consciousness of society and of his relationship to it are never for long out of his thoughts; and in the end, of course, he returns to his "good town," where he finds it pleasant "to have someone to talk to instead of speaking only to himself and to the sea." To go no further than Santiago's isolation, therefore, or to treat it, as Weeks does, as a theme in opposition to Hemingway's concern with society is to miss the deepest level of significance both in this novel and in Hemingway's writing generally.

For, surely, as Edgar Johnson has shown, the true direction of Hemingway's thought and art from the beginning and especially since 1937 has been a return to society—not in terms of any particular social or political doctrine, but in the broad sense of human solidarity and interdependence. If he began by making "a separate peace" and by going, like Santiago, "far out" beyond society, like the old man, too, he has come back, through Harry Morgan's " 'no man alone,' " Philip Rawlings's and Robert Jordan's "no man is an island," and Santiago's "no man is ever alone on the sea," with a deepened insight into its nature and values and a profound awareness of his relationship to it as an individual.[9]

In the process, strangely enough—or perhaps it is not strange at all—he has come back from Frederic Henry's rejection of all abstract values to a reiteration for our time of mankind's oldest and noblest moral principles. As James B. Colvert points out, Hemingway is a moralist: heir, like his world, to the destruction by science and empiricism of nineteenth-century value assumptions, he rejects equally these assumptions and the principle underlying them—that intellectual moral abstractions possess independent supersensual existence. Turning from the resulting nihilism, he goes to experience in the actual world of hostility, violence, and destruction to find in the world which destroyed the old values a basis for new ones—and it is precisely here,

[9] This development in Hemingway's thought and art is further illustrated in a story which he wrote in 1939 and which, prompted by the recent Cuban revolution, *Cosmopolitan*, CXLVI (April, 1959), 4, 78–83 has reprinted. "Nobody Ever Dies!" is the story of a Spanish-speaking young man and a girl who have given themselves with selfless devotion to the cause of social liberty in a revolt in Cuba. The young man is trapped and killed by governmental forces, and the girl faces the torture of questioning with "a strange confidence. It was the same confidence another girl her age had felt a little more than five hundred years before in the market place of a town called Rouen."

Colvert suggests, in reflecting the central moral problem of his world, that Hemingway is a significant moralist.[10]

But out of this concern with action and conduct in a naturalistic universe, Hemingway has not evolved new moral values; rather, he has reaffirmed man's oldest ones—courage, love, humility, solidarity, and interdependence. It is their basis which is new—a basis not in supernaturalism or abstraction but hard-won through actual experience in a naturalistic universe which is at best indifferent to man and his values. Hemingway tells us, as E. M. Halliday observes, that "we are part of a universe offering no assurance beyond the grave, and we are to make what we can of life by a pragmatic ethic spun bravely out of man himself in full and steady cognizance that the end is darkness." [11]

Through perfectly realized symbolism and irony,[12] then, Hemingway has beautifully and movingly spun out of an old fisherman's great trial just such a pragmatic ethic and its basis in an essentially tragic vision of man; and in this reaffirmation of man's most cherished values and their reaffirmation in the terms of our time rests the deepest and the enduring significance of *The Old Man and the Sea*.

[10] James B. Colvert, "Ernest Hemingway's Morality in Action," *American Literature*, XXVII (Nov., 1955), 372–85.

[11] E. M. Halliday, "Hemingway's Ambiguity: Symbolism and Irony," *American Literature*, XXVIII (March, 1956), 3.

[12] Halliday's comment on Hemingway's ironic method is particularly applicable to *The Old Man and the Sea:* "the ironic gap between expectation and fulfilment, pretense and fact, intention and action, the message sent and the message received, the way things are thought or ought to be and the way things are—this has been Hemingway's great theme from the beginning; and it has called for an ironic method to do it artistic justice" (*ibid.*, p. 15).

Hemingway's Extended Vision:
The Old Man and the Sea

by Bickford Sylvester

Cleanth Brooks wrote recently that the early story, "Fifty Grand," "presents Hemingway's basic theme quite as well as *The Old Man and the Sea*." "Nor do I think," he continued, "that Hemingway in his most recent story now finds the world any more meaningful than he once found it." [1] For once Mr. Brooks was following rather than initiating opinion. Ever since *The Old Man and the Sea* was published, critics have admitted that in its effect upon the reader the book is somehow different from Hemingway's earlier work. Those who like the difference and those who do not have tried to account for it in many ways, most of them familiar to readers of the early reviews and of the surprisingly few later readings of the story. But to a man commentators have assumed that whatever the story's new impact—whatever the nature of that affirmative power most readers have felt—it reflects no essential change in Hemingway's view of an inscrutable natural order in which, ultimately, man can play no part. [2] I want to suggest, on the contrary, that *The Old Man and the Sea* reveals Hemingway's successful achievement at last of a coherent metaphysical scheme—of a philosophical naturalism which, although largely mechanistic in principle, embraces the realm of human affairs and gives transcendent meaning to the harsh inevitabilities Hemingway has always insisted upon recording.

"*Hemingway's Extended Vision:* The Old Man and the Sea" *by Bickford Sylvester. From* PMLA, *LXXXI (March, 1966), 130–38. Copyright © 1966 by the Modern Language Association of America. Reprinted by permission of the Modern Language Association of America.*

[1] *The Hidden God: Studies in Hemingway, Faulkner, Yeats, Eliot, and Warren* (New Haven, 1963), p. 14.

[2] It is only fair to say that Leo Gurko has provocatively referred to the world of the story as "no longer a bleak trap . . . but a meaningful integrated structure": "*The Old Man and the Sea,*" CE, XVII (October, 1955), 14. Yet this suggestive remark is unfortunately so undeveloped as to be enigmatic, and I am reluctant to classify it.

I think it is precisely the failure to recognize the presence of this informing scheme that has hampered the most searching students of the story. And what is equally important, I think this oversight largely accounts for several recent interpretative extremes. On the one hand we have Clinton S. Burhans with his well-intentioned portrayal of the aging Hemingway as an apologist for conventional views of human solidarity,[3] and on the other hand we have Robert P. Weeks supporting the *Encounter* critics by insisting that because the style and attitude of *The Old Man and the Sea* is different from that in Hemingway's earlier work, the book is a fuzzy-minded failure, inferior to the first short stories.[4]

Therefore, let me work into my analysis of the story by at least attempting to answer Mr. Burhans, whose article has been reprinted by Carlos Baker[5] and is often discussed in the classroom. In referring to Santiago's apology for having "gone out so far," [6] Burhans argues that the old man's sin is specifically that of "isolated individualism in a universe which dooms such individualism" (p. 447). But Santiago's has been a necessary transgression, says Burhans, because in the story "only through the isolated individualism and the pride which drive him beyond his true place in life does man develop the qualities and the wisdom which teach him the sin of such individualism and pride" (p. 453). Like Hemingway himself, Burhans thinks, Santiago has had wrongfully to withdraw from the social community in order finally to appreciate the old values of "human solidarity and interdependence" (p. 451). But rather than the homogeneously interdependent community Burhans posits, in which individualism must be viewed ironically, there are the passive dependents and the active, tested individuals, as always before in Hemingway's works. Indeed, the distinction in the story between those who break the way for themselves and

---

[3] *"The Old Man and the Sea:* Hemingway's Tragic Vision of Man," *AL,* XXXI (January 1960), 446–55. Further references are included in my text.

[4] "Fakery in *The Old Man and the Sea," CE,* XXIV (December 1962), 188–92. Falling prey to the same logic, Philip Toynbee grows shrill as he reviews comment in *Hemingway and His Critics,* ed. Carlos Baker (New York, 1961): *The Old Man and the Sea* "is meretricious from beginning to end, . . . the archaic false simplicities of its style are insufferable, . . . the sentimentality is flagrant and outrageous and . . . the myth is tediously enforced." See *Encounter,* XVII (October 1961), 87. Dwight Macdonald agrees in "Ernest Hemingway," *Encounter,* XVIII (January 1962), 121: *The Old Man and The Sea* is simply "The Undefeated," "transposed from a spare, austere style into a slack, fake-biblical style which retains the mannerisms and omits the virtues" of the earlier work.

[5] In *Hemingway and His Critics,* pp. 259–68, and *Ernest Hemingway: Critiques of Four Major Novels* (New York, 1962), pp. 150–55.

[6] Ernest Hemingway, *The Old Man and the Sea,* The Scribner Library (New York, 1952), p. 110. Further references will be included in my text accompanied by the designation *OMAS.*

those who depend upon others has been clearly identified by Leo Gurko. As Gurko points out, among all the living creatures in the story, including the men, those who are fearless and aggressive are conspicuously portrayed as clean, beautiful, and aesthetically satisfying in their behavior. On the other hand, the "hateful," "bad smelling" scavengers (*OMAS*, pp. 107–8) are uniformly disgusting, dishonest, and awkward.[7] Now the guilt for which Santiago apologizes cannot be that of individualism if individualism is the only mode of behavior sympathetically portrayed. Nor, conversely, can interdependence be the positive norm if it is also evil and dirty.

Then there is a second fundamental error in Burhans' thesis. He insists that "the theme of solidarity and interdependence pervades the action and provides the structural framework within which the old man's heroic individualism and his love for his fellow creatures appear and function" (p. 447). Yet according to most readings—all of which are true, Burhans allows—the basic structural principle of the story is that of natural parallels to man's experience. Thus no framework essentially human in focus, as is Burhans', can include the deepest origins of the story's meaning. We are presented, then, not with a pragmatic ethic spun "out of man himself," as Burhans remarks (p. 455), quoting E. M. Halliday,[8] but specifically out of man's experience of the rest of nature.

The community element should therefore be considered as a motif somehow ancillary to the theme of natural precedence which accounts for the rich complexity of the story. Burhans' primary assumption, of course, is that Hemingway has increasingly turned from his earlier concern with the universals of nature to concentrate upon the relations between men (p. 447), and he cites *For Whom the Bell Tolls* as indicative. Still convinced of the inscrutability of the universe, Burhans thinks, Hemingway has settled, finally, for the warmth that men can derive from each other. If an objective appraisal of *all* of *The Old Man and the Sea* establishes anything, however, it is that this particular direction in Hemingway's thought and art has reversed since *For Whom the Bell Tolls*. If the theme of the novel is that "no man is an island," the theme of the story is that man*kind* is not an island. The idea can be found in the Old Testament sermon from which Hemingway took the title of his first novel: "For that which befalleth the sons of men befalleth / beasts; even one thing befalleth them; as the one / dieth so dieth the other; yea, they have all one / breath; so that man hath no pre-eminence above a / beast" (Ecclesiastes iii.19). Long ago Hemingway declared of social concerns in general: "Let those who

---

[7] Gurko, p. 12.
[8] "Hemingway's Ambiguity: Symbolism and Irony," *AL*, XXVII (March 1956), 3.

want to save the world if you can get to see it clear and as a whole." [9]
And I think that the serenity which readers find new in *The Old Man
and the Sea* springs from Hemingway's discovery at last of a quintessential natural truth which gives meaning to all struggles, including
man's.

What is this essential perception, then, and how does it reconcile
Santiago's individualism with the passivity of the shallow water fisherman? There is indeed in *The Old Man and the Sea* a greater tolerance
shown toward the total community than ever before in Hemingway's
work. Burhans, like many reviewers,[10] is right in perceiving this much.
But rather than interdependence, there is implied the dependence of
the many upon the one, of the passive community upon a potent individual redeemer who, in his dependence upon a principle basic to
universal order, is independent of all men. This is the implication of
the Calvary allusions and it is, furthermore, consistent with the individualism stressed by the system of natural parallels throughout the
story. Without going into extensive illustration, I want to outline
what I mean.

A careful study of the behavior of the creatures Santiago encounters
at sea reveals an affirmation of the values of strength, total immersion
in activity, and the exploitation of adversity. Several species include
exceptional individual members whose aggression and desire for intensity of experience lead them to oppose natural manifestations. Thus
the great marlin turns against the Gulf Stream as soon as he is hooked
(*OMAS*, p. 45), and refuses to yield to the current until the moment of
his death. Yet his blue stripes, the color of the sea, reveal that in his
paradoxical opposition to the sea he is closer to her than are the brown
surface fish who always swim with the current.[11]

Accordingly, the other champions of the story, who each bear the
color of the sea, also inherit a defiance of their mother's whims. The
blue-eyed Santiago (*OMAS*, p. 10), who has only his hands between
himself and the sea (no buoys or machines [*OMAS*, p. 29]), only the
food the sea proffers (*OMAS*, p. 27), and whose very sun-cancer is sig-

[9] *Death in the Afternoon* (New York, 1932), p. 148.

[10] See especially Robert Gorham Davis' review in *The New York Times Book
Review,* 7 September 1952, p. 1, and J. Donald Adams, "Speaking of Books," *The
New York Times Book Review,* 21 September 1952, p. 2.

[11] The carefully reported navigational details of the marlin's progress, scru-
pulously distinguishing as they do between the direction in which he is facing
and the direction in which he is actually moving at key points in his run, reveal
that the current, moving at a speed greater than his and at a forty-five degree
angle to his initial heading, gradually peels him off to the east (*OMAS*, pp. 45,
46–47, 53, 67, 84, and 86). His heading in relation to the current is thus presented
as a gauge of his vitality. And the fact that he comes up to die when he is at
last facing exactly in the direction of the flow suggests that for him congruence
with nature is tantamount to death, just as opposition to her equals life.

nificantly benign (*OMAS,* p. 9), also demonstrates that the sea bestows her greatest favors upon those who make their own conditions. Like the marlin, the blue-backed Mako shark who "would do exactly what he wished" (*OMAS,* p. 101), and the golden dolphin who shows purple stripes when he is "truly hungry" enough to take any risk (*OMAS,* p. 72), Santiago opposes the sea when her vagaries conflict with his purpose. He crowds the current (*OMAS,* p. 33), and he gladly risks the dangerous hurricane months in which, significantly, the biggest fish are to be had (*OMAS,* p. 61).

Indeed, by a chain of associations pervading the texture of the story, opposition to nature is paradoxically revealed as necessary to vitality in the natural field upon which the action takes place. Both the marlin and the "September" fisherman are old (*OMAS,* pp. 41 and 18), oriented away from that phase of the life cycle when the natural sources of energy flow freely. But the greater concentration thus required of them yields the greater intensity which is an indication of life itself.[12] All implications accrue, eventually, to expose a fundamental natural principle of harmonious opposition. Hence flow subsidiary motifs which can also best be stated as oxymorons: compassionate violence, comfortable pain, life in death, aged strength, and victorious defeat. These provide the structure of the story.

Each of the exceptional individuals of the various species has something "strange" about his eyes (*OMAS,* pp. 14, 96, and 101) which suggests his perception of the paradoxical logic of nature.[13] Acting accordingly, each adopts a mode of behavior which leads ultimately to his death in an intense contest with a champion from another species. But upon this contact, which always leads to impossible odds for one, depends the vital interplay of nature, as I shall explain presently. "I killed the shark that hit my fish," says Santiago, suggesting the vital round (*OMAS,* p. 103). And Santiago, because of his acceptance of the terrible odds, is able to become "the towing bitt" (*OMAS,* p. 45), the

[12] Santiago has always had a significant affinity for the evening sun: "It has more force in the evening too. But in the morning it is painful" (*OMAS,* p. 33). Attuned to the strenuous purity of experience objectified by the intense evening light, he finds the unconcentrated and diffuse morning light alien and distasteful.

[13] Santiago remarks, "Once I could see quite well in the dark. Not in the absolute dark. But almost as a cat sees" (*OMAS,* p. 67). This reference to relative darkness reverberates in the "blackness," the diminution of corporeal sight, that later overcomes Santiago as he kills the marlin, yet permits the glimmer of spiritual insight which (as I shall consider presently) is his reward for having immersed himself in opposition to nature. Such insight is, of course, beyond the "younger fishermen," who never extend themselves against the sea. It is their conventional vision, in which the sea as mother should reward an exploitative relationship based upon passive cooperation with her moods and currents, that leads them to deny her maternity—to speak of her as masculine—because she disappoints their expectations (*OMAS,* pp. 29–30).

essential link, between humanity and the natural world. Christlike, he must "cushion the pull of the line" with his body (*OMAS*, p. 77). Like the marlin, and the Mako who is also part of the scheme, he bears in calm solitude the terrible brunt of the only genuine communion with nature, and thus in his agony he redeems the unextended ones, the shallow water fishermen who make up most of the human race. The parasitical surface fish and the scavenger sharks, of course, fill out the rest of the other two species involved in the circular scheme.

Very subtly, then, the rationale emerges in which Hemingway is at last able to see some transcendent purpose in the stringent individualism he has hitherto regarded, bleakly, as an end in itself. It is a rationale, I think, in which the exceptional performer's position is secure enough to permit his serene acceptance of his fellows. The majority was not born to be like him and yet, dependent upon him, it has its place in the world. Thus, I suggest, we can account for Santiago's compassionate understanding of the shallow water fishermen, without forcing ourselves to ignore the positive emphasis upon exceptional achievement pervasive in the story.

Indeed, it is entirely wrong to regard Santiago's individual experience as valuable only as a lesson in the folly of isolated activity, and to suggest, therefore, that Santiago's reward comes at the end of his journey as he rejoins the community. For Santiago's reward comes, not on land but at the farthest point in his circular voyage, at the moment of his greatest isolation from other men. It comes when he plunges his lance into his quarry.

As Santiago concludes his awesome chase, the fish leaps high out of the water and dies. The marlin seems at the summit of his death leap "to hang in the air" above his slayer (*OMAS*, p. 94). Surely this is another of the moments of cessation occurring at the high points in the circular experiences of all Hemingway's major heroes, and serving to define the achievement of transcendent experience. Yet the point has not been commented upon. Frederic I. Carpenter, in a discussion of intensified experience in Hemingway's work generally, has noted that Santiago's realistic performance of the "ritual techniques of his trade," and his subsequent identification of "the intensity of his own suffering with that of the fish," contribute to an "occasional mysticism" in the story.[14] Some attention to the moment of the marlin's death, however, would have given greater point to Carpenter's thesis. For as the fish seems to Santiago to hang "motionless in the sky" before it falls

[14] "Hemingway Achieves the Fifth Dimension," *PMLA*, LXIX (September 1954), 717. Cf. two subsequent analyses of Hemingway's use of time: Keiichi Harada, "The Marlin and the Shark: A Note on *The Old Man and the Sea*," in *Hemingway and His Critics*, pp. 274–76, and Earl Rovit, *Ernest Hemingway* (New York, 1963), pp. 130–46 esp.

(*OMAS*, p. 98), the old man is (like Robert Jordan when he feels the "earth move out and away" from him and Maria)[15] undergoing a sensation of timelessness in time—an ecstatic perception of what Carpenter calls the "eternal now." Santiago "was sure there was some great strangeness and he could not believe it" (*OMAS*, p. 98). The contest in which Santiago has been engaged is presented as a pattern of action in time so exactly in accord with what has always happened everywhere that there is no discrepancy between the immediate enactment and the eternal act. As the "now" and the perpetual become fused, relativity ceases; thus for the participants in the action all sensation of motion disappears. Santiago's reward for his struggle is, therefore, not in the nature of a lesson at all. It is that Lear-like perception of the eternal which the very rare creature can wrest from the round of existence, the one boon that cannot be reclaimed by the sea which has provided it.

But what is of greater importance is that Santiago's moment of "strangeness" marks the first time in Hemingway's major fiction in which the experience of ultimate participation culminates a hero's main endeavor. There are Jake Barnes' peaceful fishing trip above Burguete, and Lieutenant Henry's idyllic winter interlude away from the war; and Robert Jordan's ecstasy occurs, of course, during a lull in his preparation for the bridge. Thus each earlier case clearly suggests that the rest of the universe operates only according to the frictionless concord implicit in moments of ideal love—as a Shelleyan cosmos, actually—and that man's manifest dedication to violence must leave him ultimately cut off from consonance with all that is universal and abiding, merely tantalized and diminished by what he has glimpsed. But Santiago's vision culminates his commitment to worldly struggle. Thus the compassionate violence implicit in his slaying of the marlin he loves is revealed as the key to a universal harmony in which man may partake. Hemingway has at last been able to employ the central paradox of the bullfight and the hunt[16] so as successfully to reconcile the

---

[15] *For Whom the Bell Tolls* (New York, 1940), p. 159. Further references will be included in my text accompanied by the designation *FWBT*.

[16] Santiago's wonder and his admiration for his victim echo especially Hemingway's description of his response to the kudo he has killed in the climactic scene of *Green Hills of Africa* (New York, 1935): cf. "I stooped over and touched [the kudo] to try to believe it" (p. 231), and Santiago's "I want . . . to touch and to feel him . . . he could not believe his size . . . he could not believe it" (*OMAS*, pp. 95–96, 98). Cf. also Hemingway's initial refusal to watch as his quarry is skinned (*Green Hills of Africa*, p. 235), and Santiago's reluctance to look at his mutilated catch (*OMAS*, p. 110).

The matador motif in the story has been discussed, in contexts different from mine, by Melvin Backman, "Hemingway: The Matador and the Crucified," *MFS*, I (August 1955), 2–11, Joseph Waldmeir, "Confiteor Hominem: Ernest Hemingway's Religion of Man," *PMASAL*, XLII (1957), 354–55, and Robert O. Stephens,

forces of love and violence which have hitherto remained ironically separated in his major works of fiction.

His achievement is partly foreshadowed by two incidents in *For Whom the Bell Tolls*. As Jordan sets up a machine gun, soon after his experience of sexual transport with Maria, she begs him to tell her that he loves her and at the same time to let her help him shoot. But Jordan still lives in the world of all Hemingway's earlier heroes, a world in which there can be no meeting ground for love and killing:

> "Dejamos. Get thee back. One does not do that and love all at the same moment."
>
> "I want to hold the legs of the gun and while it speaks love thee all in the same moment."
>
> "Thou art crazy. Get thee back now." (*FWBT*, p. 270)

Only in the last chapter of the novel, just before he crosses the fatal road, does Jordan learn better.

> He had never thought that you could know that there was a woman if there was battle; nor that if there was a woman that she should have breasts small, round and tight against you through a shirt; *nor that they, the breasts, could know about the two of them in battle.* But it was true and he thought, good. That's good. (*FWBT,* p. 456, italics mine)

It is good because it means that under certain conditions violence and love turn on the same axis, that the course of Jordan's return to

---

"Hemingway's Old Man and the Iceberg," *MFS,* VII (Winter 1962), 301–2. Backman (p. 10) calls attention to some similarities between the moment of the marlin's death and that of the bull's, but there are several specific details he overlooks. The calm deliberateness of both man and fish gives the entire conclusion of the struggle a ritualistic quality; Santiago's foreknowledge and premeditation of his every act, especially once the fish starts to circle, make his execution of the last stage of the combat as stylized and inevitable as that of the *faena.* The fish has been guided from his original position one-hundred fathoms away through progressively tighter circles until he is made to pass close by the old man several times, much as the bull is drawn in by the matador during the final series of passes (see Stephens, p. 302). As the two figures are at last united, the man directs his weapon behind the great chest fin that rises "into the air to the altitude of the man's chest" (*OMAS,* p. 94). At the crucial moment, then, each reaches for the other's heart, as do the matador and the bull—the one with the sword and the other with the menacing horn. And the description of the death-thrust itself (when in accord with the story's theme of complete extension Santiago can touch the marlin's heart—achieve a union of love—only by pushing a second time on the shaft [*OMAS,* p. 95]) verbally echoes a celebrated passage in *Death in the Afternoon.* Cf. "He felt the iron go in and he leaned on it and drove it further and then pushed all his weight after it" (*OMAS,* p. 94), and "The beauty of the moment of killing is that flash when . . . the sword goes all the way in, the man leaning after it" (*Death in the Afternoon,* p. 247).

worldly entanglement does not lead away from the meaningful continuity of the universe, but is only another part of its endless flux. Jordan's thoughts at this point mark a major advance in Hemingway's work, I think, for they express the insight which is modified and developed in *The Old Man and the Sea.* Jordan seems to realize as he lies alone at the end of the novel that by killing "to prevent something worse from happening to other people" (*FWBT,* p. 380) he is, in effect, committing an act of love.[17] And as he presses himself against the forest floor, his eyes fixed on the white clouds (*FWBT,* p. 471), there is the suggestion that he is once again caught up in natural order as he had been when making love to Maria.

Yet his violent delaying action against the fascists is to be, after all, not in itself an act of love, but an act in the service of love. Clearly Jordan's second feeling of consonance with nature is but a reward for his championship of the blissful ideal which informs the love scene. His experience is emphatically more intense in the earlier scene than in the later one. It is not until *The Old Man and the Sea,* therefore, when Hemingway shifts his focus from human affairs to the vital contact between species—and between the creatures and the rest of nature—that he manages to compress the bases for Jordan's separate mystical experiences into a single culminative moment.

Now the fact that Hemingway is able at last to see the world "clear and as a whole" only by perceiving that love and violence may be simultaneously expressed—and that in order to do so he has had to replace the protective aspect of Jordan's love by Santiago's sense of identification with a respected adversary—leaves his new conception obviously vulnerable to all sorts of value judgments. His vision of something rather like a cosmic bull ring invites us to question whether there are not metaphysical, social, and even biological complexities which cannot be crowded into such an arena.[18] But I am concerned here with the specific way in which Hemingway extends *his* view of reality so as to discover a harmony between human and natural affairs as he sees them. And there is evidence beyond his published work that Hemingway was preoccupied during the last of his productive period with employing the paradoxical fusion of affection and violence more centrally in his fiction than he ever had earlier. In 1951 Professor

[17] Cf. Theodore Bardacke, "Hemingway's Women," in *Ernest Hemingway, The Man and His Work,* ed. J. M. McCaffery (Cleveland, 1950), p. 350: the love between Jordan and Maria is "of the social conflict rather than in opposition to it."

[18] The role of procreative love would seem to be both threatened and threatening, for example. This is an implication, not only of the present study, but of Verne H. Bovie's searching analysis of the male and female principles in Hemingway's work. See "The Evolution of a Myth: A Study of the Major Symbols in the Works of Ernest Hemingway," unpubl. diss. (Pennsylvania, 1955), Ch. viii esp.

Harry Burns of the University of Washington read manuscripts of *The Old Man and the Sea* and of the novella now tentatively entitled *The Sea Chase,* one of the series of works that we have heard Hemingway originally intended to publish with *The Old Man and the Sea.* Professor Burns has given me permission to report that Hemingway had been working back and forth between these other units and *The Old Man and the Sea* intermittently for ten years. He had indeed thought of publishing the whole group together. And *The Sea Chase,* the other unit most nearly in finished form in 1951, dealt with an anti-submarine captain in the Caribbean whose animosity toward an enemy submarine commander developed into grudging admiration and finally into love, even as he intensified a deadly pursuit of his unseen undersea victim. The thematic parallel to *The Old Man and the Sea* is striking, of course.

But to return to *The Old Man and the Sea* itself, Santiago's epiphany is not our only indication that in their tense struggles the champions in the story act in accord with natural order. The marlin's fight lasts exactly forty-eight hours; it is seventy-two hours, from morning to morning, between Santiago's departure and his resurgence of vitality at the story's end; and another great primitive up against invincible odds, the "Great negro from Cienfuegos" whom Santiago defeats in "the hand game," struggles just twenty-four hours even—from dawn to dawn (*OMAS,* pp. 68–70). Thus the champions' ordeals achieve temporal synchronization with the larger units of natural order. Furthermore, the marlin's "strange" death occurs at noon. He dies at the crest of a leap as the sun is at its apex. And we are reminded that for the sun, too, the moment of defeat is also one of supreme victory.[19] The sun also falls, but like the marlin, the Negro, and the fisherman, it has lasted all the way around. Nor can we forget the shape of Santiago's entire sea-journey, far out to the moment of brief stasis in which victory and defeat are in fleeting balance—and then the return to port. This temporal and spatial coincidence between the journey of the sun and the various rounds of combat implies consonance with an order which is supra-animate—which is universal in the observable physical world.

Moreover, the emphasis upon temporal completion suggests specifically that nature sanctions the champions' intuitive maintenance of a precise degree of intensity—the source of that good pain, "the pain of life" (*OMAS,* p. 116), which comes to Santiago *"easily* and *smoothly"* (*OMAS,* p. 67, italics mine).[20] The marlin's aggressive

---

[19] It is perhaps worth remembering also that while Christ did not die at noon, His ordeal began then, as does the marlin's, and that the observers of His death also had a strange vision.

[20] See also *OMAS,* p. 64: Santiago is "comfortable but suffering" as he rides out

reaction to the current is tempered by his calmness. He does not seek brief balance, but a prolonged approximate balance. Rather than run himself out in a futile flurry as do lesser fish (*OMAS*, p. 60), or break the line and immediately free himself, Hemingway makes clear (*OMAS*, p. 63), he seems to accept his inevitable sacrifice and, like Santiago against the sharks, seek rather to endure than to prevail—to last a certain amount of time while fighting all the way. It is this ideal degree of force—not great enough to end the tension, and yet enough to keep up as much tension as possible—which earns him his harmony with the sun, and which emerges as the final dynamic principle of natural perpetuity. (The fishing line, stretched just under the break- ing-point throughout the chase, is a suggestive symbol.) The fish has left just enough strength for his great leap as he dies, and Hemingway remarks, "Then the fish came *alive,* with his *death* in him" (*OMAS*, p. 94, italics mine). The marlin has found the most intense life in this kind of death—in having lasted all the way around while retaining enough strength to meet the final thrust of the harpoon with the same resolute aggression he has shown toward the stream and the weight of the boat.

And the sharks are to the man what the man and current have been to the fish. Led by the champion shark, they are the final overwhelm- ing natural odds against which a champion must pit himself. As they do their work Santiago's material gain and his strength are eaten away as had been the marlin's heading against the Gulf Stream, so that the reader feels a parallel between the old man's continued struggle after his marketable take is gone and the marlin's stubborn resistance even when he is turned "almost east" with the current (*OMAS*, p. 84). But like the fish the man has paced himself. He fights the sharks until "something" in his chest is broken (just as the fish's heart had been pierced by the harpoon) and he notices the "coppery" taste of his blood in his mouth (*OMAS*, p. 119). Yet even at the end of the story, as he tells the boy of his broken chest, he undergoes a resurgence of life and plans another trip. He, too, comes alive "with his death in him." He will die. That is why the boy is "crying again" as he leaves the old man sleeping (*OMAS*, p. 126). Death is the final concomitant of life in a champion's combat with nature. And the only reason Santiago's death is not portrayed within the story is that his heart, like that of the great

---

the last night of the chase. Further emphasis upon the ultimate harmony im- plicit in intense suffering is subtly embodied in minor statements of the Calvary motif. "*Rest gently* now against the wood," Santiago tells himself as he huddles in the bow (*OMAS*, p. 66, italics mine); and the great Negro's hand is described as having been forced down until it "rested on the wood" (*OMAS*, p. 70). In the context of this story, of course, Christ is seen to have been comfortable in His agony. Cf. Backman, pp. 10–11.

turtle he loves, will continue to beat "for hours after he has been cut up and butchered" (*OMAS*, p. 37).

But what matters is that as a champion he has contributed to the order of the universe: that like the great creatures he has opposed he possesses innate qualities which have permitted him to bring his struggle to cyclical completion without relaxing the tension of life even though he has felt his death in him.[21] I doubt that Hemingway could have found a more felicitous representation of this orderly opposition of forces than the twenty-four-hour hand-game which ends the great Negro's competitive career. As we have observed at length, the mechanistic principle of life objectified in that scene reverberates throughout the story. It insinuates itself kinesthetically into our nerves and muscles as we read. And this is what accounts, I suggest, for much of that extraordinary artistic impact which has for so long intrigued interpreters and eluded definition.

Clearly, then, the value of the rare act is found in the act itself, not in a reaction against it, as Burhans' thesis demands, nor even primarily in its power to inspire others in the community or yield satisfaction for its participants, as Earl Rovit has suggested.[22] Such an act—such a life —on the part of its exceptional creatures is valuable as the only means whereby each species is permitted its contribution to the systematic tension of the universe. And this contribution is the object of that mythic quest which Rovit quite rightly perceives in Santiago's journey.[23]

The sin for which Santiago apologizes, therefore, is not that of having left his "true place in the world," as Burhans claims (p. 453). Yet contrary to Rovit's feeling,[24] there is an element of tragic sin in the story. There is the suggestion that Santiago's slaying of the marlin and his responsibility for its mutilation are sins, and that they are tragic precisely because they are a necessary result of his behavior as a champion of his species. In Hemingway's work, generally, the destruction of beauty is a sin. We are reminded of the rhetorical question in *Death in the Afternoon:* "Do you know the sin it would be to ruffle the arrangement of the feathers on a hawk's neck if they could never be replaced?" [25] And within the context of *The Old Man and the Sea* Santiago's sin is even greater. For he has destroyed the huge fish's power of opposition, his spiritual as well as his physical beauty. Santiago does not want to look at the fish after the sharks have started their attack

[21] We notice here that the champion shark also "would not accept" his death, and plowed over the water after being fatally stabbed (*OMAS*, p. 102).

[22] *Ernest Hemingway*, pp. 89–90.

[23] Ibid., p. 88.

[24] Ibid., p. 90.

[25] P. 159.

because, "drained of blood and awash he looked the colour of the silver backing of a mirror and his stripes still showed" (*OMAS,* p. 110). The association with a mirror, which reflects whatever is before it, suggests complete passivity; and the stripes still show to remind Santiago that this champion once was predominantly blue, bright with the color of opposition. At the end of the story the lifeless tail of the great fish who has so resolutely battled the powerful current lifts and swings "with the tide," and his stripped skeleton waits "to go out with the tide" (*OMAS,* p. 126). Santiago has rendered his respected adversary devoid of autonomy in a world where autonomy is the supreme virtue.

Indeed, the old man's human consciousness of his guilt, his awareness that in order to be right he must also be wrong, is the most formidable obstacle to resolution which he encounters during his voyage. Perhaps this uniquely human handicap is the hampering "bone spur" Santiago ponders as he thinks of DiMaggio: "Maybe we have them without knowing of it," he reflects (*OMAS,* p. 97). At any rate, it is the one valid element of humanism in the story. In overcoming it Santiago demonstrates the one thing "that a man can do" that is not duplicated by the other natural aristocrats. In this limited sense the story can be seen as profoundly humanistic, as a modern parable of man's fallen state in which the universe requires man to overcome more in order to achieve what is necessary for all creatures.[26] But no reading should ignore the fundamental emphasis upon natural aristocracy which alone gives the book its value as a commentary upon man.

It is therefore unfortunate that Burhans, who is the only critic to direct sufficient attention to the concept of necessary sin in *The Old Man and the Sea,* is led astray by his need to make Hemingway into something he is not. Burhans' approach may please those who are resigned to the absence of supernaturalism in great contemporary works, but who will not accept the pragmatic ethic they find in such works unless it happens to support the traditions of western humanism. Hemingway suffers as much from the rationalizations of such critics as he does from those of the Marxists.[27] For although man may be in the foreground he is not the measure of Hemingway's final world, and uniquely human qualities do not provide the norms of that world.

[26] Although restrictive, such a conception of human uniqueness adequately accounts, I think, for the provisional title "The Dignity of Man," which Carlos Baker reports Hemingway to have considered for the story. See Baker's introduction in the collection, *Three Novels* (New York, 1962), p. vii. Nor should we overlook Hemingway's probable awareness of the implication that man is most dignified when he accepts and exploits in himself those traits most universal in nature.

[27] For a recent discussion of the humanists' reservations about Hemingway see John A. Yunck, "The Natural History of a Dead Quarrel: Hemingway and the Humanists," *SAQ,* LXII (Winter 1963), 29–42.

That is why Hemingway remained primarily fascinated by those rare men whose talents spring from their natural superiority rather than from their methodical application of experience. In the last published work of his lifetime, his magazine account of the contest between the matadors Dominguin and Antonio Ordoñez, Hemingway demonstrated his new-found tolerance and made a statement which might seem to bear out the contention that he had indeed abandoned his exclusivism. Contemplating a foolish chauffeur who once tried to make the sign of the cross a substitute for skill, Hemingway recalled: "Then I thought again and remembering . . . the need for solidarity in this passing world I repeated his gesture." [28] But the whole account of the contest itself turns upon a qualitative distinction between Dominguin, a skilled and intellectual performer, and Ordoñez, who is "a natural." Hemingway is first escorted to Ordoñez by a very successful matador: "Jesus Cordoba is an excellent boy and a good and intelligent matador and I enjoyed talking with him. *He left me at the door of Antonio's room.*" [29] With characteristic understatement, of course, Hemingway was suggesting the almost mystical reverence with which he observed a separation between the intelligent man and the natural rarity. Then, precisely echoing his description of another great man—and a marlin and a shark—he said, "I noticed the eyes first . . . those strange eyes." [30] Hemingway had mellowed, but he had abandoned nothing. He had simply moved forward.

What is new in *The Old Man and the Sea,* let me repeat, is Hemingway's discovery that the need for extended effort in the face of inevitable darkness is not merely a man-made hypothesis, not a masochistic sop to the unmoored human ego, but the reflection of a natural law man is permitted to follow. The idea of an immanent order based upon the tension between opposed forces is in one formulation or another a familiar one, of course. We think of Heraclitus, and Hegel, as well as of more recent philosophers.[31] But the idea has perhaps

[28] "The Dangerous Summer," Part I, *Life,* 5 September 1960, p. 94.
[29] Ibid., p. 86 [italics mine].
[30] Ibid.
[31] For example, the following remark by J. Novicow is especially relevant to the synthesis I have attributed to Hemingway: "The apologists of war are quite right in this, that struggle is life. Struggle is the action of the environment upon the organism and the reaction of the organism upon the environment, therefore a perpetual combat. . . . Without struggle and antagonisms societies would indeed fall into a state of somnolency, of most dangerous lethargy." See *War and its Alleged Benefits,* trans. T. Seltzer (New York, 1911), pp. 102–3, and quoted by Pitirim A. Sorokin in his *Contemporary Sociological Theories* (New York: Harper Torchbook, 1964), pp. 315–16. Novicow specifically departs from the quintessential vision of *The Old Man and the Sea,* however, when he adds: "Besides the physiological struggle, humanity has economic, political, and intellectual struggles, which do not exist among animals. It may even be stated that the physiological

never been so consummately concretized in a work of art as it is in *The Old Man and the Sea,* where its presence is in all likelihood almost entirely a product of Hemingway's life-long observation of man and nature. The order with which Santiago achieves consonance is indeed limited to the natural world. But within the observable physical universe of this story man is seen to play his part in a way which has not yet been sufficiently articulated by any critic.

We can see a way, then, in which Mr. Weeks is wrong to be disturbed by the several errors in factual observation in the story. Hemingway is working here partly with new artistic means to match his new vision. Formerly, convinced of the absence of a perceptible order in the world, Hemingway made a fetish of presenting objects exactly as they appeared, so that any latent meaning could shine through them without distortion. But here, convinced of the principle behind the facts, he can occasionally take poetic license and present objects for any kind of associational value they may have. Mr. Weeks thinks it merely a lazy error on Hemingway's part, for example, that Rigel, the first star Santiago sees one night, actually appears close to midnight in the Caribbean.[32] But Rigel, after all, is a first-magnitude star in the constellation of Orion, the hunter. And it is entirely appropriate, symbolically, to call attention to Santiago's attunement with the stars in this way. Hemingway is in this story at last attempting to pull the world together, rather than to reveal its ironic division. Thus "the way it was " need no longer be his sole guide as an artist.

If we are accurately to assess Hemingway's total achievement—and it is now our responsibility to begin that task—we must recognize that he was a writer who neither abandoned nor helplessly parodied his essential vision, but who significantly extended it, finding in paradox and symbolism the artistic means to do so.[33] However we may evaluate

---

struggle, the dominant form in the animal kingdom, has ended among men, since they no longer eat one another" (p. 103). For recent and variant views of the psychological and sociological significance of struggle see Herbert Marcuse, *Eros and Civilization* (Boston, 1955), and Norman O. Brown, *Life Against Death* (Middletown, Conn., 1959).

[32] Weeks, p. 192.

[33] Perhaps, indeed, in suggesting that Hemingway's essential method is a restrained, realistic exploitation of irony (rather than the free use of symbolism Carlos Baker finds), Mr. Halliday has confused matters by opposing symbolism and irony (Halliday, p. 22). I have assumed that it is *paradox* and irony which are appropriately opposed devices, differing in the direction of their operation—paradox stressing an unexpected unity between things conventionally considered different (as I have shown in discussing *The Old Man and the Sea*), and irony emphasizing unexpected differences between things conventionally considered together (as in Hemingway's earlier work). Symbolism, on the other hand, merely has to do with representation, I should think, and depending upon its use can emphasize either distinction or identification, either division or unity. For other

his advance, we must severely qualify our tendency to regard him as
the champion of mindlessness in literature.[34] For we have evidence in
the last great published work of his lifetime that either consciously or
unconsciously he eventually became as concerned with perfecting what
he had to say as he had always been with polishing his way of saying it.

---

objections to Halliday's approach see Bern Oldsey, "The Snows of Ernest Hemingway," *WSCL*, IV (Spring-Summer 1963), 195–98 esp. The issue is a significant
one, as Philip Young has remarked in an evaluation of recent Hemingway criticism: "Our Hemingway Man," *KR*, XXVI (Autumn 1964), 695.

[34] The most forthright recent assertions of Hemingway's intellectual emptiness
are those of Toynbee and Macdonald: Hemingway "had no extractable views
on man's nature and destiny which bear a moment's scrutiny" (Toynbee, p. 87);
"his one great talent" was for "aestheticism unsupported by thought or feeling"
(Macdonald, p. 121). For succinct arguments supplementing the evidence I have
presented against the validity of this persistent critical assumption see Baker's
introduction to *Hemingway and His Critics*, pp. 14–18, and Rovit, pp. 165–73.

The Old Man and the Sea
and the American Dream

by Delmore Schwartz

The Old Man and the Sea, Hemingway's most recent novel (1952), is not so much a masterpiece in itself as a virtuoso performance, a new demonstration of the novelist's gifts far more than a new development of them. The experience of literature is always comparative; Hemingway's sixth novel has almost the same theme as *The Undefeated,* a story written twenty-five years before, and the old fisherman who has not made a catch for eighty-four days is in the same human situation as the aging matador of that story. Compared with that and other stories, and with the best episodes in Hemingway's previous novels, there is a certain thinness of characterization and situation.

Yet *The Old Man and the Sea* does give a new definition and meaning to Hemingway's work as a whole. It gives the reader an intensified awareness of how, for Hemingway, the kingdom of Heaven, which is within us, is moral stamina alone, and experience, stripped of illusion, is inexhaustible threat. It is completely clear in this novel, as it is not when his characters are expatriates in Europe, that Hemingway's primary sense of existence is the essential condition of the pioneer. It is above all the terror and isolation of the pioneer in the forest that Hemingway seeks in his prize fighters, matadors, soldiers, and expatriate sportsmen. The old man's solitude is also meaningful: apart from the brief appearance of the young boy who is devoted to him, sorry for him, and has been told to avoid him, Santiago is the only human being in a narrative more than one hundred pages in length! The giant marlin is a sympathetic character for whom the old man develops a certain fondness and the sharks who destroy all but the marlin's skeleton are villains whom he detests: the astonishing fact

"The Old Man and the Sea *and the American Dream" [Editor's title] by Delmore Schwartz. From "The Fiction of Ernest Hemingway: Moral Historian of the American Dream," in* Perspectives USA, *No. 13 (Autumn, 1955), 82–88. (Entire essay 70–88.) Copyright 1955 by Intercultural Publications, Inc. Reprinted by permission of Kenneth Schwartz.*

remains that one human being is enough to make a genuine narrative. Moreover the old man is not only alone physically, but since he is old he will always be alone, cut off from youth, hope, friendship, love, and all the other relationships which sustain human beings. Hence, as the old man struggles with the sea—with time, nature, and death— he possesses a singular purity of will and emotion. The completeness of his solitude does much to relate the novel to all of Hemingway's work, making one more aware of how some form of solitude isolated every other leading character, giving a new clarity to Jake Barnes' mutilation, Frederick Henry's "separate peace," the solitude which the shell-shocked Nick Adams seeks on a fishing trip in *Big Two-Hearted River*, and the monologue of the dying writer in *The Snows of Kilimanjaro*. Thus, in a way, the old fisherman is the quintessential hero of Hemingway's fiction. Other human beings are simply absent now, and only the sharks are present to interfere with the naked confrontation of man and nature. It is the solitude which requires absolute courage and complete self-reliance.

With the old fisherman the pattern of Hemingway's fiction has come full circle. The hero as an old man stands in clear relation to the hero as a young boy and Nick Adams as a child in *Indian Camp*, the first story of Hemingway's first book. In that story Nick goes with his father, a doctor, to witness the mystery of birth: but he witnesses the horror of death also. The young Indian woman his father has come to help has been in labor for two days. "Daddy, can't you give her something to stop the screaming?" Nick asks his father. The doctor tells his son that despite her outcry the woman wants to be in labor and pain because she wants to have the baby and the baby too wants to be born. Then Dr. Adams performs a Caesarean using a jackknife. Dr. Adams feels exalted as he goes to tell the woman's husband the operation was successful—and finds him dead. His wife's screaming has made the Indian kill himself. This is hardly the initiation Dr. Adams had intended for his son. Yet, as father and son row home across the lake, Nick's reassurance grows as his father replies to his questions about suffering and death. As the sun rises over the lake Nick feels "sure that he would never die." This sentence illustrates the extreme illusion about existence which is native to the Hemingway hero and which makes disillusion, when it occurs, so astonishing and disastrous.

Just as the birth of a child causes the death of a man in *Indian Camp*, so in the last chapter of *A Farewell to Arms*, not only does the birth of a child cause the heroine's death, but before her death when she cries out in her agony, she speaks exactly like Nick Adams: "Can't they give me something?" and Frederick Henry says to himself: "She can't die," just as Nick was sure that he would not die. When the heroine dies, the burden of the hero's experience of birth, love, and death is a characterization of the nature of existence:

> So now they got her in the end. You never got away with any-thing . . . You did not know what it was about. They threw you in and told you the rules and the first time they caught you off base they killed you . . . They killed you in the end . . . You could count on that. Stay around and they would kill you.

The first illusion is that one will not die. The essential disillusion is death. Hence without exception every Hemingway hero suffers serious physical wounds, often as an initiation to the disillusion of reality and the ultimate wound of death.

The exact parallel of detail which links *Indian Camp* and the last chapter of *A Farewell to Arms* ought not to conceal an emotional difference which is quite important. Nick's primary illusion about existence in the first story, though it is shaken by his direct encounter with the reality of the agony of birth and suicide, is quickly restored: he concludes, as he began, with the same illusion that he will never die. Frederick Henry in *A Farewell to Arms* concludes in disillusion and despair. He has made a separate peace not only with war and love, but with life itself. Santiago in *The Old Man and the Sea* sur-passes both prior characters. He suffers neither from illusion nor disillusion: he lives, as he says, by hope: "It is silly not to hope," he tells himself, and "besides, it is a sin." His kind of hope is clearly very different from Nick's return to illusion and Frederick Henry's sur-render to disillusion. The passage from illusion through various phases of disillusion to the conclusion of sober hope represents the novelist's profound spiritual and emotional progress during the thirty years of his career.

The Capital of the World (1936) is perhaps one of Hemingway's most illuminating stories. The hero, a young waiter, gets killed in a pointless accident while practicing "the great media-veronica" of the matador. This is the author's comment and conclusion:

> He [the young waiter] died, as the Spanish phrase has it, full of illusions. He had not had any time in his life to lose any one of them, nor even, at the end, to complete an act of contrition . . . he had not even had time to be disappointed in the Garbo film which disappointed all Madrid for a week . . . The audience disliked the Garbo picture thoroughly . . . they were intensely disappointed to see the great star in miserable and low surroundings when they had been accustomed to her surrounded by great luxury and brilliance.

This is the most complete description of illusion in Hemingway and at the same time the most extreme statement of despair. Since the loss of illusion can only be prevented by early death, the only available anesthetic is the opium of death. This is as far as it is possible to travel from the belief that one will never die without believing in suicide. And it is a further indication of the immense experience of suffering which Hemingway's fiction encompasses. The vision of experience as pain, the imagination of suffering of every kind, requires a quality of compassion and sympathy on the author's part which seldom has been recognized.

Despair can only be known after the disappointment of hope; disillusion can only occur after the experience of illusion. The primary illusion in *The Capital of the World*—and the same illusion in all Hemingway's fiction—is illustrated by the reference to Greta Garbo in a Hollywood film. But the primary illusion and hope existed long before Hollywood, and it has often been called the American Dream. Hollywood has popularized and vulgarized the American Dream so widely, that its true character and dignity has become somewhat obscured. It is formulated in the American Constitution as every human being's inalienable right to life, liberty, and the pursuit of happiness.

The American Dream is believed by many human beings who, like Hemingway's disillusioned characters, are unaware of their belief or convinced that they have awakened from it. The fact, which must be pointed out once more, that disillusion is inseparable from illusion and despair from hope, is disregarded. The right to happiness as the law of the land is the belief by which Hemingway's most desperate and unhappy characters live when they drink, travel, and play games. Like many more sanguine human beings, they have converted the legal right to life, liberty, and happiness into attitudes, emotions, an organized way of life which believes not only in the pursuit but the certainty of happiness. The American Dream converts the pursuit of happiness into the guarantee of a happy ending. For some this is promised by the nature of reality; for far more, it is supported by the nature of America as the New World where all are equal. And the American Dream is so primary and so important as a source of illusion and hope that the dream becomes insomnia when it is not fulfilled, or in a like way, courage is needed solely to cope with the unbearable pain of disappointment. Hemingway's fiction bears the same witness as the essential substance and avowed faith in the writings of Emerson, Thoreau, Whitman, and Melville.

The Hemingway hero's attitude toward himself and toward existence depends immediately upon the American Dream. Thus the first onset of disillusion is one in which the hero as a young man persuades the heroine to have an abortion: "We can have everything," the heroine says, "if we get married." "No, we can't," the hero answers, "it isn't ours anymore . . . Once they have taken it away, you never get it back." And when he adds this brief description of himself, "You know how I get when I worry," the heroine agrees to the abortion, thus: "If I do it you won't ever worry?" because never to worry is part of the dream. And when disillusion becomes despair, when the stock market crash begins a depression which seems unending, Hemingway, as his own hero, hunting big game in Africa feels that he is through with America since the American Dream has ended:

> A continent ages quickly once we come . . . The earth gets tired of being exploited . . . *A country was made to be as we found it.* Our people went to America because that was the place to go then. It had been a good country and we had made a bloody mess of it and I would go, now, somewhere else as *we always had the right to go some-where else.* Let others come to America who did not know that it was too late . . . I knew a good country when I saw one. Here there was *game, plenty of birds . . . Here I could hunt and fish.*

Hemingway's sentences have been italicized to demonstrate that the pioneer and the immigrant and the hunter and fisherman are identical in the Hemingway hero whenever he thinks of how to regain the dream, and now how like Huck Finn he can always "light out for the frontier."

When the American Dream seems to have collapsed once and for all, the Hemingway hero (in *To Have and Have Not*) loses an arm smuggling to keep his family off the relief rolls, and decides that the heroic individual no longer has a chance by himself. And although the Hemingway hero has made a separate peace and said a farewell to arms years back, he goes to fight for the Loyalists in Spain because, as he says, he believes in life, liberty, and the pursuit of happiness, thus identifying the Spanish Civil War and the American Revolution: one man alone has a chance, after all, to save humanity and hence the hero, Robert Jordan, blows up a bridge as a way of firing a shot which will be heard around the world. Robert Jordan's father has killed himself because of the Wall Street stock market crash, just as Nick Adams' father has committed suicide because, being a sentimental man, he was always being betrayed. And every American of Hemingway's generation has known the most exalted expectations and the most desperate disasters. Living through the First World War, the great era of prosperity, the crash, the long depression, the Second World War, and a new era of prosperity, he has been subjected to the American Dream's giddy, unpredictable, magical, tragic, and fabulous juggernaut. It is thus natural enough that the Hemingway hero should always feel threatened, always in danger, always subject to what the sociologists call "status panic." A society committed to the American Dream is one which creates perpetual social mobility but also one in which the in-

dividual must suffer perpetual insecurity of status as the price of
being free of fixed status. Hence the Hemingway hero is always afraid
of failure, no matter how often he has succeeded, which is precisely
what the old fisherman says: "'I will show him what a man is and
what he endures' . . . The thousand times that he had proved it meant
nothing. Now he was proving it again. Each time was a new time." This
is the reason that the Hemingway hero must continually assert his
masculinity: he may always lose it, as he may always lose his strength,
his youth, his health, his skill, his success, and thus his sense of selfhood.

Of all modern novelists it is Hemingway who has written the most
complete moral history of the American Dream in the twentieth century: the greatest of human dreams is the beginning of heartbreaking
hope and despair; its promise is the cause of overwhelming ambition
and overwhelming anxiety: the anxiety and the hope make courage
an obsession and an endless necessity in the face of endless fear and
insecurity: but the dream, the hope, the anxiety, and the courage began with the discovery of America.

PART TWO

View Points

Frederick I. Carpenter

In "The Bear," perhaps, the American myth has received its most conscious fictional embodiment. And in Hemingway's *The Old Man and the Sea,* the same struggle with wild nature, the same defeat, and the same mysterious achievement of grace occurs again. In both, the myth appears in all its ambiguity. The American Adam kills the wild thing that he loves, but learns thereby a deeper wisdom. Achieving a new maturity, he does not reject all innocence, but consciously chooses a wiser innocence. Destroying the primitive, he recognizes his kinship with it also. Losing paradise, he glimpses a paradise to be regained.

Earl Rovit

Structurally, the *novella* follows the traditional pattern of the quest or the journey. Santiago has an unexplainable "call" or vocation to be a fisherman and to meet the marlin in the deep water. Mythically he has no real choice in the matter; he has been ordained for this one encounter: "Perhaps I should not have been a fisherman, he thought. But that was the thing that I was born for." And this is not a quest to be taken lightly. Santiago is not just a fisherman, he is The Fisherman—the one chosen from all the others because of his superior merits of skill and character. Manolo, who suggests the superiority of Santiago's fishing abilities, hints also that the encounter will demand something more than being merely a great fisherman: *"Qué va,"* the boy said. "There are many good fishermen and some great ones. But there is only you." The movement from *type* to *archetype* is prefigured. The great marlin will not come to a great fisherman; he will only be caught by a great Man. In Emersonian terms, Santiago is valuable because he is not a fisherman, but Man-Fishing; and Santiago's soliloquies in the skiff in which he sees his profession in organic relationship to the rest of life bequeath to his ordeal something more than exceptional competence and stamina. As he rests against the bow on the second night, he welcomes the appearance of the first stars:

> He did not know the name of Rigel but he saw it and knew soon they would all be out and he would have all his distant friends.
> "The fish is my friend too," he said aloud. "I have never seen or heard of such a fish. But I must kill him. I am glad we do not have to try to kill the stars."
> Imagine if each day a man must try to kill the moon, he thought. The moon runs away. But imagine if a man each day should have to try to kill the sun? We were born lucky, he thought. . . .
> I do not understand these things, he thought. But it is good that we do not have to try to kill the sun or the moon or the stars. It is enough to live on the sea and kill our true brothers (75).

As he fights the fish—a solitary old man with a straw hat desolate on the great sea—he is not in any real sense alone at all. A literal cord joins him to his "brother," the fish. Other equally strong cords bind him to the "things" of nature—the sun, the moon, and the stars; the sea life and the birds; his town, his neighbors, the boy, and his past. It is as "whole" man that he meets the fish and brings him back; and it must be as Man, not fisherman, that his experience be measured.

However, even though Santiago has been "chosen" as representative champion to go on this quest, he must be put in readiness for it. For eighty-four days his endurance to withstand failure is put to the test; he must be made "definitely and finally *salao*, which is the worst form of unlucky," before his vigil is ended. And then he must go "far out," "beyond all people in the world," to find what he seeks. The quest hero must be set apart from men and from their daily pursuits—the results of the baseball games and the gossip of the men of the fishing wharves—because immersion in the regularities of the commonplace will dull his spiritual readiness. He must receive his final rites of purification far out in the wilderness, beyond the glow of lights from Havana. He must be tortured with pain and hunger and thirst; he must be reduced to naked will and the capacity to reflect. And then, when he is thoroughly ready, the last barrier is stripped off. He loses for a moment—a barely perceptible but determining moment—his precious sense of individuality. His will remains through the pure momentum of his determination, but the "he" that began the voyage becomes lost:

You are killing me, fish, the old man thought. But you have a right to. Never have I seen a greater, or more beautiful, or a calmer or more noble thing than you, brother. Come on and kill me. I do not care who kills who.

Now you are getting confused in the head, he thought. You must keep your head clear. Keep your head clear and know how to suffer like a man. Or a fish, he thought (92).

This is the final requisite for success in the quest. In this moment Santiago loses Santiago, merges into his struggle with the fish, merges into the fish and the universal struggle of life, and becomes elemental Man and quest hero.

But this successful catch, this angling vision into the heart of mysteries, can not be brought back whole to the community of men. As they must, most men spend the greatest part of their lives enwrapped in a world where prudence and practicality are the measurements of *what is*. Living within the blanketing hum of everyday reality with solid earth beneath their feet, men cannot see what they have no eyes for, nor can they understand what they have not been prepared to understand. The tourists who mistake the marlin's skeleton for that of a shark are not especially culpable; there is no reason why they should have known the difference, just as most men cannot discern the difference between the gleam in a maniac's eye and that in a saint's or a mystic's. The kind of experience which Santiago undergoes is an incommunicable one, but it is not without value to the community of men. He has been a champion of mankind for men and not for himself. He has brought back from his isolation a fragmented gift offering to his fellows, an imperfect symbol to suggest where he has been and what he found there. There are those within the community with the experience and the imagination and the necessary love to project on that skeletal symbol a feeling of the experience which it represents. For them the world has been redeemed; a shaft of knowing has pierced like a thunderbolt into their awareness of what it is to be a man and the image of mankind has been immeasurably enhanced. And through them the experience will be filtered down to the others who are less sensitive or less prone to enflesh the mysteries. It will suffer dilution and diffusion as it is passed along, changing into legend, into folk story, into barely remembered anecdote. But the ripples of the great marlin's dive will radiate in ever-expanding circles, and each of the community of men will be the measure of what he can find there.

I have taken pains to suggest that there is no tragic quality to this myth, and that Santiago is neither saint nor martyr. He loses three hundred dollars worth of marlin, he suffers great pain and severe tribulation, but he is never shaken at his inner center by his deprivation. He is a man; he does what he is born to do; and, in doing it, he achieves *being*. He decides that he was beaten because he went out too far; but it is difficult to believe that he *is* beaten, and it was necessary for him to go out "too far" in order to catch what he had to catch. He has far too much humility to be seen as an "over-reacher," just as he has too much love for his antagonist to sit well in a Promethean role. In fact, the pervasive equanimity that is such a marked characteristic of *The Old Man and the Sea* keeps it, I think, from breaking through into the realm of great tragic poetry that rests just one layer lower beyond the reach of Santiago's harpoon.

Malcolm Cowley

At cocktail parties you already hear the book described as the poor man's *Moby Dick*. Some variation of that remark is now being applied to every living author, painter or composer; one will be the poor man's Dante, another the poor man's El Greco or Mozart, and the remark itself is becoming the poor man's epigram. In the present instance it is justified by a surface resemblance in plot, but by absolutely nothing in the essence of the two books. *Moby Dick* is still our greatest novel and the other is a long story; if they illuminate each other—and they do—it is only by contrast.

Where *The Old Man and the Sea* is classical in spirit, *Moby Dick* is quintessentially romantic; it accepts no limits of any sort. The hero, Captain Ahab, is so lofty in his pride and vengeance that he rises above our common humanity, or sinks beneath it. The white whale is not merely the largest of living creatures but becomes a sort of deity immanent in nature, "the great gliding demon of the seas of life." Demon and titan, whale and whalesman, are described in a fashion that strains the resources of the English language, as if the author, like Captain Ahab, were in perpetual pursuit of the never attainable.

Hemingway's hero, instead of being a titan, is an old man reduced to living on food that is begged or stolen for him by a teen-age boy. He is even "too simple to wonder when he had attained humility," but he still takes pride in his skill and resolution as a fisherman. Therefore, when his luck turns bad, he goes farther out into the Gulf Stream than anyone else from his village had dared to go alone. The fish that takes his bait is not a great gliding demon, a natural force personified,

From "Hemingway's Novel Has the Rich Simplicity of a Classic" by Malcolm Cowley. Review of The Old Man and the Sea, New York Herald Tribune Book Review, XXIX, No. 4 (Sept. 7, 1952), 1, 17. Copyright © 1952 by the New York Herald Tribune. Reprinted by permission of the author.

but simply the largest and noblest of the marlin. There is no hint in the story of Melville's essentially romantic feeling that God is immanent in man and nature. When the old man prays it is to an orthodox god transcending nature, but he and the fish are both in nature; they are even brothers in nature.

*   *   *

I couldn't write even a short report on the book without paying tribute to Hemingway's prose. It is as different from Melville's prose in *Moby Dick* as anything could be and still remain English. There is no attempt in it to express the inexpressible by inventing new words and turns of phrase; instead Hemingway uses the oldest and shortest words, the simplest constructions, but gives them a new value—as if English were a strange language that he had studied or invented for himself and was trying to write in its original purity. A typical passage among dozens I would like to quote tells how the old man caught the small tuna that he would eat to keep him strong:

> He dropped his oars and felt the weight of the small tuna's shivering pull as he held the line firm and commenced to haul it in. The shivering increased as he pulled in and he could see the blue back of the fish in the water and the gold of his sides before he swung him over the side and into the boat. He lay in the stern in the sun, compact and bullet-shaped, his big, unintelligent eyes staring as he thumped his life out against the planking of the boat with the quick shivering strokes of his neat, fast-moving tail.

At first we don't think of the passage as good narrative prose or any kind of prose; we think of the tuna that thumps his life out; something is happening before our eyes and the prose seems to be merely a transparent medium for revealing it. On second reading, however, we begin to notice patterns in the transparency. The words are short, with one exception, and all of them are familiar, but there are little shocks of freshness in the way the words are combined, as in "neat, fast-moving tail." "Shivering" sets the musical tone of the passage and is used three times. The one long word is "unintelligent" and its value is revealed by its being set in shorter words like a big turquoise in silver.

Hemingway has a peculiar manner of typing: in his manuscripts each word is separated from the following by three or four spaces. That may be the result of a defective space bar on his typewriter, but I like to believe that it has something to do with his feeling that each word has a special value and should stand out separately and cleanly on the page. That is what the words seem to do in *The Old Man and the Sea*. The writing has the quality of being familiar and yet perpetually new that is the essence of classical prose.

I remember reading about one of Louis XIV's courtiers, a consummate horseman who believed that his art was best displayed, not in cantering or galloping or jumping, though he excelled in all, but simply by walking his horse across the courtyard at Versailles; it was by so doing that he displayed his ease, his perfect seat, his mastery of the steed. There is something of the same spirit in *The Old Man and the Sea*. One could never say that it was Hemingway at a walk, since that would imply that he was relaxed, whereas the story is tense, concentrated and full of excitement; but it is Hemingway displaying his strength and richness in simplicity.

Leslie A. Fiedler

The Old Man and the Sea returns to a level of technical accomplishment almost equal to the earlier work by stripping away all social implications and any attempt to deal with mature emotions. Hemingway is always less embarrassing when he is not attempting to deal with women; and he returns with relief (with what we as readers at least feel as relief) to that "safe" American Romance of the boy and the old man. The single flaw in *The Old Man and the Sea* is the constant sense that Hemingway is no longer creating, but merely imitating the marvelous spare style that was once a revelation; that what was once an anti-rhetoric has become now merely another rhetoric, perhaps our most familiar one, and that even its inventor cannot revive it for us.

From Chapter *13*, *"Adolescence and Maturity in the American Novel"* in An End to Innocence: Essays on Culture and Politics *by Leslie A. Fiedler (Boston: Beacon Press, 1955), p. 194. Copyright © 1955 by Leslie A. Fiedler. Reprinted by permission of Beacon Press.*

Nemi D'Agostino

Certainly the exotic and primitive setting of the tropics in *The Old Man and the Sea* is better suited to Hemingway's aged hero than is the new Europe. The main theme of the story is absolute failure in life and the irrational sublimation of the defeat. The saintly Santiago goes back in the end to his dreams, his head almost encircled with the halo

From *"The Later Hemingway"* by Nemi D'Agostino, *trans. Barbara Melchiori Arnett.* The Sewanee Review, LXVIII *(Summer, 1960), 491–92. (Entire essay 482–93.) Copyright © 1960 by The University of the South. Reprinted by permission of* The Sewanee Review.

of holiness. The old man is certainly not the brother of the great realistic heroes of Tolstoy or Verga, nor is he, on the other hand, a fully convincing character in the tradition of symbolism. The story leaves the realistic level as soon as Hemingway tries to make it something more than an immediate objective reality, the moment the strange old man begins to accompany the action with a lyrical commentary, using a refined oratorical language, emphasizing its symbolical substratum, its nature as a projection of the poet's consciousness. As soon, that is, as the chase itself stands revealed as an exploit springing from *un élan d'infini, un amour de l'impossible,* The fable contains a subtle anagogy, which unfortunately is more imposed from without than an intrinsic part of it. Whatever the old man is intended to symbolize (and he seems to be a biblical and Melvillean version of the usual Hemingway hero) he simply does not come poetically true; the symbolism remains a fictitious disguise, and the religious or mystical implications are forced insofar as they want to be more than the religion and morality of aestheticism.

Actually the rhythm and idiom of the tale is a clue to its essential emotion. The rhythm is the cadence of the lyrical paragraph, which proceeds with a sumptuous and solemn fall. The language is rich in suggestive and exotic words, in rich and sensuous imagery, in highly literary expressions, in bright and exquisite touches, and is consciously regulated by a love of verbal magic. It is, in short, the rhythm and language of a decadent *poème en prose,* which, however suggestive and intense, must always remain an artificial and minor form, incapable of full historical and moral significance. Within these limits *The Old Man* is certainly a refined work, with its admirable linear development and its brilliant "imagistic" style. A late work by a tired writer who believes more than ever in the religion of beauty, its subtly mannered idiom, its elegant and frozen rhythms, are separated by the space of a whole lifetime from the lucid movement, the fresh and crystalline clarity, the poignancy and the shock-power of the language of the young Hemingway.

Robert Gorham Davis

Santiago's simplicity together with the articulateness of his soliloquies sometimes makes him seem a personified attitude of his complex

From "Hemingway's Tragic Fisherman" by Robert Gorham Davis. Review of The Old Man and the Sea, The New York Times Book Review *(September 7, 1952), Section 7, 20. (Entire review pp. 1, 20.) Copyright 1952 by* The New York Times Company. *Reprinted by permission of* The New York Times Company *and Robert Gorham Davis.*

creator rather than a concrete personality in his own right. The action is wonderfully particularized, but not the man to whom it happens and who gives it meaning. The talk of baseball, of the "great Di-Maggio" and the "Tigres" of Detroit does not help in this.

Philip Rahv

Hemingway's new story happily demonstrates his recovery from the distemper that so plainly marked his last novel, *Across the River and Into the Trees*. In *The Old Man and the Sea* the artist in him appears to have recouped some of his losses, curbing the overassertive ego so easily disposed to fall into a kind of morbid irritability of self-love mixed with self-pity. It is to be hoped that the recovery is more than temporary.

But free as this latest work is of the faults of the preceding one, it is still by no means the masterpiece which the nationwide publicity set off by its publication in *Life* magazine has made it out to be. Publicity is the reward as well as the nemesis of celebrities, but it has nothing in common with judgment. Though the merit of this new story is incontestable, so are its limitations. I do not believe that it will eventually be placed among Hemingway's major writings.

Moreover, it is in no sense a novel, as the publishers would have us believe. At its core it is actually little more than a fishing anecdote, though one invested with an heroic appeal by the writer's art, which here again confirms its natural affinity with the theme of combat and virile sports. This art is at its best in the supple and exact rendering of the sensory detail called for by its chosen theme; and in telling of the old fisherman's ordeal on the open sea—of his strenuous encounter with a giant marlin, the capture of him after a two-day struggle, and the loss of the carcass to the sharks in the end—Hemingway makes the most of his gifts, turning to good account the values of courage and endurance and discipline in action on which his ethic as an artist depends.

The premise of the story—its moral premise at any rate—is the purity and goodness and bravery of Santiago, the Cuban fisherman. And given Hemingway's habitual attitude of toughness coupled with sentimentality, one can easily make out the chief threat to the integ-

Review of The Old Man and the Sea *included with a review of* Across the River and Into the Trees *in "Hemingway in the 1950's," Part VI of "Sketches in Criticism,"* Image and Idea: Twenty Essays on Literary Themes, *rev. and enlarged ed., by Philip Rahv (New York: New Directions Publishing Corp., 1957), pp. 192–95. Copyright 1952 by Philip Rahv. Reprinted by permission of New Directions Publishing Corporation.*

rity of the writing; and it is in fact to the circumvention of sentimentality that the story owes its success. The two scenes (in which the boy displays his adoration of Santiago) that are not quite exempt from the charge of sentimentality are but indirectly related to the action. They form a lyrical prelude and postlude to the action, which is presented in fictional terms that are hard and clear. And it is saved from false sentiment by Hemingway's wonderful feeling for the sea and its creatures—a feeling that he is able to objectify with as much care and devotion as he lavishes on the old man. This creates the rare effect of our perceiving the old man and the fish he catches as if they existed, like a savage and his totem, within the same psychic continuum. No wonder that at the height of his battle with the fish Santiago exclaims: "You are killing me, fish. . . . But you have a right to. Never have I seen a greater, or more beautiful, or a calmer or more noble thing than you, brother. Come on and kill me. I do not care who kills who."

When all this has been said, however, one is still left with the impression that the creative appeal of this narrative is forceful yet restricted, its quality of emotion genuine but so elemental in its totality as to exact nothing from us beyond instant assent. It exhibits the credentials of the authentic, but in itself it promises very little by way of an advance beyond the positions already won in the earlier phases of Hemingway's career. To be sure, if one is to judge by what some of the reviewers have been saying and by the talk heard among literary people, the meaning of *The Old Man and the Sea* is to be sought in its deep symbolism. It may be that the symbolism is really there, though I for one have been unable to locate it. I suspect that here again the characteristic attempt of the present literary period is being made to overcome the reality of the felt experience of art by converting it to some moral or spiritual platitude. It goes without saying that the platitude is invariably sublimated through the newly modish terms of myth and symbolism. As Lionel Trilling reported in a recent essay, students have now acquired "a trick of speaking of money in Dostoevsky's novels as 'symbolic,' as if no one ever needed, or spent, or gambled, or squandered the stuff—and as if to think of it as an actuality were sub-literary." Perhaps this latter-day tendency accounts for the inflationary readings that Hemingway's story has received, readings that typically stress some kind of schematism of spirit at the expense of the action so lucidly represented in its pages. Hemingway's big marlin is no Moby Dick, and his fisherman is not Captain Ahab nor was meant to be. It is enough praise to say that their existence is real, and that their encounter is described in a language at once relaxed and disciplined which is a source of pleasure. In art, as Wallace Stevens once put it, "Description is revelation. It is not / The thing described, nor false facsimile." And I would suggest to the ingenious interpreters that they look to the denotations of a work of literature before taking off into the empyrean of pure connotation.

Philip Toynbee

You either believe or you do not believe that the book is meritricious from beginning to end, that the archaic false simplicities of its style are insufferable, that the sentimentality is flagrant and outrageous and that the myth is tediously enforced.

*   *   *

The Old Man and the Sea might be described as a long short story; but it marks no return at all to the special talents which Hemingway had so long ago abandoned. It is a stuffed book—stuffed with the burden of all the theses which had been written about Hemingway's message and philosophy. The demands which it makes on us are crudely "literary." In fact it sounds like that penultimate note of a musical scale which creates a sense of intolerable incompletion in our ears. What must follow, of course, are the hundred exegeses. The book is doctor-bait, professor-bait. And the modern critic of Hemingway should read this nonsense carefully and then re-read *The Killers* or *The Undefeated*. Let us by all means be respectful towards each other, but I cannot believe that any sane critic would fail to see what has happened in the long interval. This is one of the genuine literary tragedies of our time.

Ernest Hemingway

If it is any use to know it, I always try to write on the principle of the iceberg. There is seven-eighths of it underwater for every part that shows. Anything you know you can eliminate and it only strengthens your iceberg. It is the part that doesn't show. If a writer omits something because he does not know it then there is a hole in the story.

The Old Man and the Sea could have been over a thousand pages long and had every character in the village in it and all the processes of how they made their living, were born, educated, bore children, etc. That is done excellently and well by other writers. In writing you are limited by what has already been done satisfactorily. So I have tried to learn to do something else. First I have tried to eliminate everything unnecessary to conveying experience to the reader so that after he or she has read something it will become a part of his or her experience and seem actually to have happened. This is very hard to do and I've worked at it very hard.

Anyway, to skip how it is done, I had unbelievable luck this time and could convey the experience completely and have it be one that no one had ever conveyed. The luck was that I had a good man and a good boy and lately writers have forgotten there still are such things. Then the ocean is worth writing about just as man is. So I was lucky there. I've seen the marlin mate and know about that. So I leave that out. I've seen a school (or pod) of more than fifty sperm whales in that same stretch of water and once harpooned one nearly sixty feet in length and lost him. So I left that out. All the stories I know from the fishing village I leave out. But the knowledge is what makes the underwater part of the iceberg.

Chronology of Important Dates

<table>
<tr><td>Hemingway</td><td>The Age</td></tr>
</table>

Early Years

1899	Birth on July 21, in Oak Park, Illinois.	
1914–18		World War I.
1917–18		U.S. in World War I.
1917	Graduation from Oak Park High School. Reporter on Kansas City *Star*.	Caporetto campaign begins in Italy. Ezra Pound, first three *Cantos*.
1918	In Italy as Red Cross ambulance driver. Wounded near Fossalta di Piave, July 8.	
1919		Treaty of Versailles. Sherwood Anderson, *Winesburg, Ohio*.
1920–24	Reporter for Toronto *Star* and *Star Weekly*.	
1920		F. Scott Fitzgerald, *This Side of Paradise*.
1921	Marriage to Hadley Richardson. First of four marriages. The others, after divorces, to Pauline Pfeiffer in 1927, Martha Gellhorn in 1940, and Mary Welsh in 1944.	

Paris Period (1921–27)— reporting, early literary success.

1921–24	Foreign correspondent for Toronto papers.	
1921–22		Graeco-Turkish War.
1922	First war correspondence in Graeco-Turkish War. Subsequent war correspondence in Spain	James Joyce, *Ulysses*. T. S. Eliot, *The Waste Land*.

(1937–39), China (1941), Europe (1942–45).

1923   *Three Stories and Ten Poems* (Paris).

1924   *in our time* (Paris).

Gertrude Stein, *The Making of Americans.*

1925   *In Our Time*—first Hemingway book published in U.S. Adds fourteen short stories to the miniatures (now interchapters) of *in our time*.

F. Scott Fitzgerald, *The Great Gatsby.*
Sherwood   Anderson,   *Dark Laughter.*

1926   *Torrents of Spring*—parody of *Dark Laughter. The Sun Also Rises* (British title, *Fiesta*)— novel.

1927   *Men Without Women*—short stories.

Key West Period (1927–38)— fishing, safari, literary experimentation.

1929–37

The Depression.

1929   *A Farewell to Arms*—novel.

Oct. 29, U.S. stock market crash.
William Faulkner, *The Sound and the Fury.*

1931

William Faulkner, *Sanctuary.*

1932   *Death in the Afternoon*—non-fiction literature, study of bull-fighting.

William Faulkner, *Light in August.*

1933   *Winner Take Nothing*—short stories. Begins *Esquire* association lasting through the 1930's.

1935   *Green Hills of Africa*—safari experience with interspersed critical reflections.

Italy invades Ethiopia.

1936–39

Spanish Civil War.

1937   *To Have and Have Not*—novel of combined short stories.

Japan invades China.

War Period (1938–45)— war correspondence in Spain, China, Europe; sub-chasing in Caribbean (Cuban residence established, 1942).

1938	*The Spanish Earth*—film script. *The Fifth Column and the First Forty-Nine Stories*—play and collected stories.	Germany invades Austria.
1939		John Steinbeck, *The Grapes of Wrath*.
1939–45		World War II.
1940	*For Whom the Bell Tolls*—novel.	
1941–45		U.S. in World War II.
1941		Dec. 7, Japanese attack on Pearl Harbor.
1942	*Men at War*—stories and articles edited by Hemingway.	
1944		Aug. 25, Allied liberation of Paris.

Cuban Period (1945–60)— renewed literary effort, return visits to Africa and Spain.

1948		Norman Mailer, *The Naked and the Dead*.
1950–53		*Korean War. McCarthy era.*
1950	*Across the River and Into the Trees*—novel.	
1951		J. D. Salinger, *Catcher in the Rye*.
1952	*The Old Man and the Sea*—novella.	Ralph Ellison, *Invisible Man*.
1954	Nobel Prize for Literature.	
1959		Cuban Revolution.
1960	"The Dangerous Summer"—study of bullfighting.	

Ketchum, Idaho (1960–61).

| 1961 | Death on July 2, of self-inflicted gun wound. | |

Posthumous.

| 1964 | *A Moveable Feast*—essays. | |
| 1967 | *By-Line: Ernest Hemingway*, ed. William White—selected news writing. | |

Notes on the Editor and Contributors

KATHARINE T. JOBES, editor of the anthology, is Assistant Professor of English at Rutgers University, where she teaches American literature and American studies.

CARLOS BAKER, Professor of English at Princeton University, is author of the critical studies *Hemingway: The Writer as Artist* and *Shelley's Major Poetry* and of the novels *A Friend in Power* and *The Land of Rumbelow*. He has edited two volumes of critical essays on Hemingway and is writing a biography of Hemingway.

CLINTON S. BURHANS, JR., Associate Professor of English at Michigan State University, is the author of *The Would-Be Writer* and essays on Hemingway, Twain, Hawthorne, and Sidney. He is co-editor of *31 Stories*.

FREDERICK I. CARPENTER, Research Associate in English at the University of California at Berkeley, is the author of many critical studies and essays, including *American Literature and the Dream, Emerson Handbook, Eugene O'Neill,* and *Robinson Jeffers.*

MALCOLM COWLEY is the editor of *After the Genteel Tradition: American Writers, 1910–1930* and *The Portable Hemingway.* He has written several studies of the literature of the 1920's and 1930's, including *Exile's Return: A Literary Odyssey of the 1920's.*

NEMI D'AGOSTINO, Professor of English Literature at the State University of Milan, is the author of *Order and Chaos, Ezra Pound,* an essay on Christopher Marlowe, and essays on several American writers in *Studi Americani,* Rome. He is currently writing a book on the post-Joycean novel.

ROBERT GORHAM DAVIS, Professor of English at Columbia University, is the author of *C. P. Snow* and *John Dos Passos.*

LESLIE A. FIEDLER, Professor of English at the State University of New York at Buffalo, is the author of *Love and Death in the American Novel,* of several collections of essays, including *Waiting for the End* and *No! in Thunder,* and of several novels and short story collections, including *Back to China* and *The Second Stone.*

LEO GURKO, Professor of English at Hunter College, is the author of *The Angry Decade; Heroes, Highbrows, and the Popular Mind; Joseph Conrad: Giant in Exile;* and *The Two Lives of Joseph Conrad.*

PHILIP RAHV, an editor of *Partisan Review,* is the author of *Image and Idea, The Myth and the Powerhouse,* and the editor of several volumes of fiction and essays, including *The Great Short Novels of Henry James* and *Discovery of Europe.*

CLAIRE ROSENFIELD, currently at the Radcliffe Institute for Independent Studies, has taught at the University of Texas and Rutgers University and has been a Fellow at the Center for Advanced Study in the Behavioral Sciences. She is the author of *Paradise of Snakes: An Archetypal Analysis of Conrad's Political Novels* and co-editor of *The Personal Voice: A Contemporary Prose Reader.* Her essays and reviews have appeared in a number of journals, including *Daedalus, Literature and Psychology,* and *Psychiatry and Social Science.*

EARL ROVIT, Assistant Professor of English at City College of the City University of New York, is the author of *Ernest Hemingway, Herald to Chaos: The Novels of Elizabeth Madox Roberts,* and of two novels, *The Player King* and *A Far Cry.*

DELMORE SCHWARTZ (1913–1966) is the author of several volumes of poems and short stories, including *In Dreams Begin Responsibilities, Summer Knowledge: New and Selected Poems, 1938–1958,* and *Successful Love, and Other Stories.*

BICKFORD SYLVESTER, Associate Professor of English at the University of British Columbia, has published essays on Shakespeare, Marvell, Wordsworth, and Hemingway. He has completed a critical study of Hemingway and is currently in England on a Canada Council Research Fellowship working on a study of "harmonious opposition" as an ordering principle in selected American Romantic literature.

PHILIP TOYNBEE, novelist and essayist, is the author of *The Barricades, Prothalamium: A Cycle of the Holy Graal, The Garden to the Sea,* and *Comparing Notes: A Dialogue Across a Generation* (with Arnold Toynbee).

ROBERT P. WEEKS, Professor of English at the College of Engineering, University of Michigan, is editor of *Hemingway* in Prentice-Hall's Twentieth Century Views series, of *Commonwealth vs. Sacco and Vanzetti,* and of *Machines and the Man.* He is the author of several essays on Hemingway.

ARVIN R. WELLS, Professor of English at Ohio University, is the author of *Jesting Moses: A Study in Cabellian Comedy.*

PHILIP YOUNG, Research Professor of English at Pennsylvania State University, is the author of *Ernest Hemingway, Ernest Hemingway: A Reconsideration, Ernest Hemingway* (University of Minnesota Pamphlets on American Writers), and many essays on Hemingway and other American writers.

Selected Bibliography

Backman, Melvin, "Hemingway: The Matador and the Crucified," *Modern Fiction Studies,* I (August, 1955), 2–11. Reprinted in corrected version in Carlos Baker (ed.), *Ernest Hemingway: Critiques of Four Major Novels,* Scribner Research Anthologies (New York: Charles Scribner's Sons, 1962), pp. 135–43; and in Carlos Baker (ed.), *Hemingway and His Critics: An International Anthology,* American Century Series (New York: Hill and Wang, 1961), pp. 245–58. Traces two dominant motifs— the matador, who contains force and releases it in controlled, yet violent giving of death; and the crucified, who takes pain—which are not perfectly blended in Hemingway's work until *The Old Man and the Sea.*

Cooperman, Stanley, "Hemingway and Old Age: Santiago as Priest of Time," *College English,* XXVII (December, 1965), 215–20. Sets *The Old Man and the Sea* in both biographical and literary contexts of the problem of aging for Hemingway.

Dupee, F. W., "Hemingway Revealed," *Kenyon Review,* XV (Winter, 1953), 150–55. A good review, centered on the character of Santiago and on Hemingway's values as revealed by Santiago.

Haradi, Keiichi, "The Marlin and the Shark: A Note on *The Old Man and the Sea,*" *Journal* Number 4 of the College of Literature, Aoyama Gakuin University, Tokyo. Reprinted in Baker, *Hemingway and His Critics,* pp. 269–76. Perceptive notes on some of the major images in *The Old Man and the Sea*—ocean, lions and bone spur, marlin and shark.

Hofling, Charles K., M.D., "Hemingway's *The Old Man and the Sea* and the Male Reader," *American Imago,* XX (Summer, 1963), 161–73. For the reader interested in a psychoanalytical reading. Studies how *The Old Man and the Sea* affects an adult male reader. Some suggestive analysis of the structure of the story.

Howard, Milton, "Hemingway and Heroism," *Masses and Mainstream,* V (October, 1952), 1–8. For the reader interested in tracing U.S. Marxist reaction to *The Old Man and the Sea.* This hostile review, criticizing the isolation of the hero from social struggle, is followed by another analysis—Annette T. Rubinstein, "Brave and Baffled Hunter," *Mainstream,* XIII (January, 1960), 1–23—which tries to take account of the popularity of *The Old Man and the Sea* in the Soviet Union. The reader might also enjoy, as a curiosity and as an illustration of imitation Hemingway, Robert Forrey, "The Old Man and the Fish," *Mainstream,* XIV (June, 1961), 31–38, a continuation of Santiago's story after the Cuban Revolution.

Schorer, Mark, "With Grace Under Pressure," *New Republic,* CXXVII (October 6, 1952), 19–20. Reprinted in Baker, *Critiques,* pp. 132–34. A good, mainly favorable early review. Includes discussion of *The Old Man and the Sea* as "nearly a fable."

Stephens, Robert O., "Hemingway's Old Man and the Iceberg," *Modern Fiction Studies,* VII (Winter, 1961–1962), 295–304. Analyzes *The Old Man and the Sea* as the culmination of one theme in Hemingway's work, "the vision of man as animal trying to transcend his animal nature."

Waldmeir, Joseph, "Confiteor Hominem: Ernest Hemingway's Religion of Man," *Papers of the Michigan Academy of Sciences, Arts, and Letters,* XLII (Ann Arbor: University of Michigan Press, 1957), 349–56. Reprinted in Baker, *Critiques,* pp. 144–49; and in Robert P. Weeks (ed.), *Hemingway: A Collection of Critical Essays,* Twentieth Century Views (Englewood Cliffs, N.J.: Prentice-Hall, Inc., 1962), pp. 161–68. Discusses *The Old Man and the Sea* as decisive in elevating Hemingway's "philosophy of Manhood" evident throughout Hemingway's work to "the level of a religion." Considers the function of the Christian symbolism in the story.

TWENTIETH CENTURY
INTERPRETATIONS

MAYNARD MACK, *Series Editor*
Yale University

NOW AVAILABLE
Collections of Critical Essays
ON